How to grow culin

HERBS
& SPICES

the natural way

Written and photographed by
Charlotte de la Bédoyère

Illuminated by Patricia Carter

An A–Z of herbs and spices

Good organic gardening
Compost
Pests and diseases
Propagation
Herbs in pots, window-boxes and containers

Designing a herb bed

Preserving herbs and spices

Henry Doubleday Research Association / Search Press

First published in Great Britain 1994

Search Press Limited
Wellwood, North Farm Road,
Tunbridge Wells, Kent TN2 3DR

in association with

The Henry Doubleday Research Association
National Centre for Organic Gardening
Ryton-on-Dunsmore
Coventry CV8 3LG

All photographs by Charlotte de la Bédoyère with the exception
of the following:
The publishers would like to thank Horticulture Research
International, Littlehampton, West Sussex, for permission to
reproduce on page 57 the photographs of *Encarsia formosa*,
Phytoseiulus persimilis, *Aphidoletes aphidimyza*, insect-parasitic
nematodes, sciarid fly, tomato moth caterpillar, vine weevil, and
red spider mite.

Thanks to English Woodlands Ltd. for the picture of the ladybird
Crytolaemus montrouzieri on page 57.

The publishers would also like to thank Microbio for their
assistance regarding 'Nemaslug' and Long Ashton Research
Station, England, for the picture of an infested slug on page 57.

The author would like to thank the many spice growers in the
Far East who willingly gave information about their spices and
allowed their plants to be photographed; also the many herb
growers, especially in Australia, who allowed her to roam
around in search of more pictures.

Illuminated capitals by Patricia Carter
Illustrations by Polly Pinder

ISBN 0 85532 751 0

Colour Separated by P&W Graphics Pte Ltd., Singapore
Printed in Spain by GRAFO, S.A. - Bilbao

Introduction

Herbs and spices have always been a priceless commodity. There is even evidence that wild herbs and spices were used by Neanderthal tribes for culinary and medicinal purposes. Much later, people cultivated and traded them. The Greeks and Romans were the first Europeans to trade in them and for many centuries carried out trade with the Far East.

By the Middle Ages, Europeans considered herbs and spices as valuable as gold and jewels and, no longer content to trade with Arab and Far Eastern countries, they began seeking their source for themselves, thereby changing the course of history in many parts of the world. Pepper, teas, nutmegs, cinnamon and cloves were among those considered worth fighting for.

It was not until the late fifteenth century that the world really opened up for the Europeans. Columbus set out in 1492 hoping to discover the spices of the Far East. Instead, he found America!

In 1498 Vasco da Gama discovered Calicut in India and the stampede for spices among the European seafaring nations had begun. The Spanish, French, Portuguese, Dutch and British all vied with each other to gain a monopoly of the spice trade, resulting in not only bloody battles amongst themselves, but often wholesale massacres of indigenous peoples.

The Dutch, through the East India Company (*Vereenigde Oostindische Compagnie*, more commonly known as the VOC), proved the most ruthless and successful, and eventually cornered most of the spice market. *En route* to the Far East, they had to sail round Africa and used what is now called Cape Town as a staging post. Some of the crew were driven to 'jump ship' in Cape Town and these Dutch settled in South Africa, thereby starting a momentous chain of events.

Contrary to some beliefs, most herbs and spices can be grown in any part of the world: the leafy herbs will grow almost anywhere, and all but a few of the spices can quite easily be grown even in colder climates.

This book deals solely with how to grow *culinary* herbs and spices; that is, those that are used to add flavouring to vegetables, meat, fish, fruit, cakes, bread, and other dishes. It does not deal with those used for drinks, teas, etc. Inevitably, in a book of this length, some plants have had to be left out, so if you cannot find your favourite herb or spice, I apologise.

Many of the plants in this book can also be used medicinally, but this, again, is not within its scope. You should never try to use plants as medicines unless you know exactly what you are doing, and never take any herb or spice in excessive quantities just because you think it has some property or vitamin you regard as being good for you.

The important thing about this book is that it tells you how to grow these plants naturally; that is, organically, without the use of chemical fertilisers, herbicides or pesticides, which are not only devastatingly destructive to wildlife and the environment, but often leave chemical residues on or in the plants themselves, the total effect of which is not yet wholly known.

Nowadays, herbs and spices can be bought everywhere, but how much more satisfying it is to grow your own natural ones. It can easily become one of the most absorbing of garden pursuits, and of course there is nothing more appetising than a kitchen redolent of the wonderful aroma of herbs and spices.

In the first part of this book you will find a range of wonderful herbs and spices to choose from, arranged alphabetically by the Latin name, and in the second a general guide to growing them organically, with hints on soil, compost, pests, designing herb beds, preserving your produce, and other useful topics.

Note: This book was ready to be printed when news came of a biological slug control, so if you have problems with slugs see pages 56–57.

Allium sativum
Garlic

Can be grown anywhere

Family *Liliaceae*
Annual
Height: 30cm (12in)
Soil: rich, well-manured, well-drained
Situation: sunny
Propagation: cloves
Main constituents: amino acids, fats, Vitamins A, B and C, volatile oil

Cultivation

If you are an avid garlic user, allocate a special sunny plot in the garden that has been well dug and drains well. Add plenty of compost and/or manure, and unless your growing season is particularly short and the weather cold you should get a good harvest. Split the bulb into cloves and plant them (tapering side up) about 5cm (2in) deep and 10–15cm (4–6in) apart in spring. Keep well weeded and the sun should do the rest. For a longer growing season, plant in autumn and cover with strawy compost. Harvest when leaves die off.

History

One wonders how cooks the world over would have managed without the *Allium* family, of which garlic and onions are the most widely used: from the Far East right through Europe and the Americas. Even in conservative England, garlic is now a common sight in shops. It is quite difficult to find recipes from the East and Mediterranean countries that do not use it!

Garlic, too, has a wealth of history. The Chinese have used it for centuries and records show that the Babylonians, too, used it around 3000BC. The folklore is endless: Hungarian jockeys used to carry garlic to prevent another horse getting in front; bullfighters wore it to prevent the bulls from charging. A Mohammedan legend says 'when Satan stepped out from the Garden of Eden after the fall of man, Garlick sprang up from the spot where he placed his left foot, and Onion from that where his right foot touched'. In India it is still used to ward off evil spirits. Throughout its history garlic has had great health-giving properties attached to it: it warded off colds and flus and even the plague. Modern research is still going on, but it shows that garlic has anti-

Garlic, one of the world's tastiest herbs, is not attractive to look at, so choose an out-of-the-way sunny spot for it.

If you have the patience, string garlic bulbs together and store them.

bacterial properties, can reduce blood pressure, cholesterol, and blood clotting, and is effective against many other diseases.

Preserving and main uses

Store by hanging the bulbs in a cool, dry place, and use individual cloves. Can be used in most savoury dishes with meat, fish, poultry and vegetables, salads and sauces. It is also extensively used in curries and Eastern cuisine.

Use peeled cloves, either finely chopped or crushed.

Allium schoenoprasum
Chives, civet, rush-leeks

Can be grown anywhere

Family *Liliaceae*

Hardy perennial

Height: 20–30cm (8–12in)

Soil: rich

Situation: lightly shaded

Propagation: seeds, division

Main constituents: essential oil, with sulphur

Cultivation

This is the smallest of the onion family and is easy to grow, either from seed, or by division of existing plants. Sow seeds in boxes or directly into the ground in fine soil.

Chives have just two requirements: rich soil and moisture. If given these they will go on for years and years. When clumps get too large, divide them every three years

or so. In mild weather they will give you a fresh supply of leaves all the year. Heavy frost will make them die back, so if you want a fresh supply all the year, pot up a clump and bring it into the house. The flowers are pretty but should be cut back to encourage leaf growth. If leaves go yellow or brown, they are lacking in either moisture or food.

Garlic chives are a strong-tasting alternative to chives.

Welsh onion.

Other varieties

Interesting alternatives are the Welsh onion (*A. fistulosum)* and garlic chives (*A. tuberosum*), both of which are perennials requiring similar cultivation. The flat leaves of garlic chives can be used and stored just like chives. However, the flavour is much stronger.

The leaves of Welsh onion, on the other hand, are thick and fleshy, with a very onion-like taste, and are best used when young.

History

Chives have grown all over the northern hemisphere for thousands of years, but unlike many other herbs they are not surrounded by endless folklore.

Preserving and main uses

Chives can be chopped and dried, or deep-frozen in small packets. Use in salads, soups, fish dishes and soft cheeses. I find them delicious in creamy scrambled eggs.

Chives.

A large, healthy clump of chives, which will shortly need dividing.

A*nethum graveolens*
Dill

Can be grown anywhere

Family *Umbelliferae*
Annual
Height: up to 1m (3ft)
Soil: any, well-drained
Situation: sunny
Propagation: seeds
Main constituents: oil of dill

Cultivation

Dill prefers sun and will grow in almost any soil. Sow the seeds directly in the ground in spring as dill does not like being transplanted (cover only lightly with soil). If you use just the leaves, there is no need to thin the plants, but if you want them to flower so you can harvest the seeds, thin them out to about 10cm (4in) apart. If you pick out the tops, side shoots will grow, but as the plants mature quite quickly, it is better to make three or four sowings a year at about fortnightly intervals. If some seeds are left to sow themselves, you will automatically get dill somewhere in the garden every year.

Pests and diseases

Dill suffers from carrot fly and carrot motley dwarf virus. Also, beware of slugs and other grubs, who seem to relish the small seedlings. Once my dill suffered from a form of wilt (*fusarium*); many of the plants just flopped and died. The roots had unusual swellings somewhat like club root. This is rare, but if it occurs, do not grow dill on that patch of soil for three or four years.

History

Dill is a native of Mediterranean countries and Southern Russia. It is

If you do not want seeds, pick off flower heads and allow leaves to sprout.

referred to in the Bible and was used by the Ancient Egyptians. In the Middle Ages it was one of the herbs used in spells against witches.

Michael Drayton, in his poem 'Nymphidia', writes:

> Therewith her vervain and her Dill
> That hindereth Witches of their Will.

Preserving and main uses

The seeds, of course, must be dried. You can also dry the leaves but, however quickly you do it, much of the lovely fresh flavour is lost. Freezing the leaves is also not very satisfactory. The leaves can be used in fish and meat dishes, cheeses, soups, pies, bread and for making dill butter. The seeds are used for pickling and to flavour vinegar.

Dill.

Hoverflies, a great pest-eating ally in the garden, love dill flowers.

Angelica archangelica
Angelica

Can be grown anywhere

Family *Umbelliferae*

Hardy biennial/perennial

Height: 2–2.5m (7–8ft)

Soil: any, but preferably rich in compost or manure

Situation: sunny but moist

Propagation: seed or by division

Main constituents: coumarins, plant acids, resin, starch, sugar, volatile oil

Cultivation

Choose a moist, semi-shady spot at the back of a bed, for no other herb and few vegetables will grow as tall as angelica.

Sow either directly in position or in pots. The seeds like plenty of light

Angelica.

and warmth for germination and should not be covered with soil.

Angelica is easy to grow and you can either treat it as a perennial (if you want to use just the leaves) by cutting the flower stalks as they develop. (If you allow the plant to flower it will die.) Otherwise you must consider it a biennial and grow new plants every year.

Sow in late summer for harvesting the following year. If you allow the seed heads to develop, the plant will usually propagate itself every year.

Angelica loves a richly manured soil. Mulch it well to help keep it moist in the dry season, as well as to keep down weeds. It makes a handsome foliage plant and could make a valuable addition to a herbaceous border.

Other varieties

Do not confuse it with *A. sylvestris*, a wild variety, which is not good to eat, but is the source of a yellow dye. Also, do not confuse it with giant hogweed (*Heracleum mantegazzianum*), which is poisonous.

History

Angelica is the giant of culinary herbs and probably originates from Syria, but is now widely grown throughout northern countries and as far north as Iceland and Lapland.

It is supposed to bloom on the feast of Michael the Archangel (hence its botanical name), but also, in legend, a vision of an archangel appeared, revealing that angelica could cure the plague. Although Christians held it in great esteem, calling it 'The Root of the Holy Ghost', the folklore associated with it goes back further still.

Wild angelica.

In Latvia, apparently, a procession takes place annually in which the country people carry angelica stems into the town to sell, chanting a chorus in a language so old that no one knows what it means!

Preserving and main uses

The leaves, stem, root and seeds can all be used in cooking.

Leaves should be chopped and dried and used in soups or stews. The stems, if used, should be cut in summer and can be candied. The seeds should be harvested when they turn yellow.

Cut the roots into medium-sized pieces and dry. The latter can be used in breadmaking (as in Norway). In Iceland the stems and roots are eaten raw.

Angelica is also used in many infusions.

Leaves.

Stems.

Seeds.

Roots.

7

Anthriscus cerefolium
Chervil

Can be grown anywhere

Family *Umbelliferae*
Annual
Height: about 60cm (2ft)
Soil: any, well-drained
Situation: part shade
Propagation: seed
Main constituents: volatile oil

Cultivation

This delicate parsley-like plant grows quickly and easily.

Sow seeds direct into the ground, but do not cover them, as they are light-sensitive; just press them into the soil.

The plants will mature quickly (six to eight weeks), so if sown in spring and allowed to flower and seed, they will produce another crop the same year. For years I had self-seeded chervil plants dotted around my rockery, until, after a very hard winter, they failed to appear.

Chervil dislikes drought conditions or too much heat. In cold climates it will easily grow in the greenhouse in winter. It can also be grown in pots indoors. You will find the flavour of the leaves is improved if the plants are grown in semi-shade.

Other varieties

There is a curly-leaved variety of chervil which requires identical cultivation.

The ubiquitous roadside plant cow parsley (*A. sylvestris*) is a close relative but should not be used in cooking.

The graceful leaves of a clump of chervil can look very decorative. The flowers are white and dainty.

History

Chervil is a native of Asia and Eastern Europe and was used by the Greeks and Romans. Culpeper lists a host of medicinal uses and says 'chervil, being eaten, doth moderately warm the stomach'.

The eighteenth-century English herbalist John Evelyn said it should always be included in salads as 'it is exceedinly wholesome, and chearing the spirits'.

Preserving and main uses

Chervil is indispensable in French cooking but it is now becoming more popular the world over. Use it in salads, soups, fish and meat dishes (especially pork). Leaves can be dried or deep frozen in small quantities but they are much better fresh. Always add it at the very end of your recipe, as extensive cooking will spoil its delicate flavour.

Chervil leaves.

Armoracia rusticana
Horseradish, mountain radish, red cole

Can be grown anywhere

Family *Cruciferae*

Perennial

Height: 60–120cm (2–4ft)

Soil: any

Situation: any

Propagation: root cuttings

Main constituents: asparagin, resin, sinigrin, Vitamin C, calcium, magnesium, sodium

Cultivation

Horseradish is one of the easiest of all herbs to grow, but as its seeds very rarely mature to a viable stage, it is best to buy a growing plant or get a piece of root from a fellow gardener.

Horseradish are nearly always sterile, but even the smallest piece of root, planted vertically, will quickly grow into a robust plant. Be careful, though: horseradish can be very invasive, so keep it under control by either digging up roots regularly or by somehow confining its growth.

You can confine it by growing it in old bottomless buckets (but this makes it difficult to harvest the roots) or making a confined bed by sinking boards of wood into the ground. Roots should be harvested when leaves die back.

Other varieties

Common horseradish is not particularly pretty, so try growing the variegated version.

Horseradish in flower.

Variegated horseradish.

Pests and diseases

The roots are rarely attacked, but the leaves often suffer from flea beetle damage; this does not, however, affect the plant's growth.

History

Horseradish probably originated in Eastern Europe but now grows almost anywhere, and is often found growing wild. The Greeks called it *Raphanos agrios* (wild radish) and found it useful medicinally, especially for curing scurvy, although they knew nothing of the existence of Vitamin C.

By the Middle Ages it was used as a condiment. Gerard wrote 'the Horse Radish, stauped with a little vinegar put thereto, is commonly used among the Germans for sauce to eat fish with and such like meates as we do mustarde'.

Preserving and main uses

Some people use the young leaves in salads, but its main use is the roots for sauces to eat with fish (it is delicious with smoked trout) and meats. Always use the roots freshly grated and do not cook them, as this will destroy some of the valuable constituents.

The roots should be stored in sand.

Grate roots before use, but beware: they are stronger than onions and can really make your eyes water.

Artemisia dracunculus
Tarragon, French tarragon, little dragon, mugwort

Half-hardy, requiring protection from frost

Family *Compositae*

Perennial

Height: up to 90cm (3ft)

Soil: well-drained, not too rich

Situation: part shade

Propagation: seeds, cuttings or root division in spring

Main constituents: essential oil

Cultivation

If you buy seed and want the more delicate variety, make sure it is *A. dracunculus* and not *A. dracunculoides* (see below). However, unless you require large quantities of tarragon leaves, I suggest you buy one or two plants and thereafter divide the roots or take cuttings. It loves warmth but not direct hot sun as its leaves will burn.

A. dracunculus is a perennial that will grow all the year round in temperate climates. In colder regions the leaves will die back after frost. It is a good idea to cover the roots with a good hay or straw mulch to protect them from frost. Better still, before it dies back, pot up one or two plants in a large container with plenty of crocks for drainage and bring it indoors so you can enjoy its delicate aroma all winter. Do not overwater.

Other varieties

The above variety is the best flavoured, but there is also Russian tarragon (*A. dracunculoides*) which is more robust and hardier.

History

French tarragon undoubtedly originated in the Mediterranean

A bed of French tarragon.

countries. Its other name, 'Little Dragon', derives from the Latin *dracunculus*.

It was used by the Ancient Greeks and records go back as far as 500BC. It came to Northern Europe much later.

In the Middle Ages they thought it increased physical stamina, so pilgrims tucked sprigs into their shoes before setting out on long, debilitating journeys.

Preserving and main uses

Only the leaves are used, and although they can be dried, they are much better used fresh. In drying the essential oil is lost.

Tarragon is a must for French cuisine, in which it is used extensively. It is the main flavouring in sauce Béarnaise, and is used in vinegars and in many other sauces and salads. Tarragon can also be frozen in ice cubes for drinks.

Tarragon leaves.

Borago officinalis
Borage, bee bread

Can be grown anywhere

Family *Boraginaceae*

Annual

Height: 30–90cm (1–3ft)

Soil: any

Situation: any

Propagation: seed

Main constituents: calcium, essential oil, mucilage, potassium, tannin

Cultivation

Borage is easily grown from seed, sown either directly in position or in pans and transplanted. The plants need plenty of room, so plant them about 30cm (1ft) or more apart. Unless you want large quantities of borage, I suggest you buy a single plant. It will grow large and, once established, will readily seed itself each year. Borage is said to be a good companion plant: strawberries and borage are mutually beneficial, and it can keep off diseases and insects from neighbouring plants. Borage attracts bees and other beneficial insects, apart from looking very pretty. It sometimes bears blue and pink flowers on the same plant.

History

Borage probably came from Syria but nowadays it grows almost anywhere and often grows wild. Its name, *Borago*, might be a corruption of the Latin *corago* (*cor*, heart, and *ago*, I bring). On the other hand, some say it comes from the Celtic word for a person of courage, *barrach*.

Sir Francis Bacon claimed that 'the leaf of Burrage hath an excellent spirit to repress the fuliginous vapour of disky melancholie'. Even earlier, Pliny said 'it maketh a man merry and joyful: which thing also the old verse concerning Borage doth testify: *Ego Borago gaudia semper ago.* I, Borage, bring alwaies courage'.

Preserving and main uses

Both the flowers and the leaves are used in salads and drinks, and can be cooked like spinach or crystallised. Both can be dried or frozen in ice cubes (see p. 62).

Borage in bloom.

Borage leaves.

apsicum spp.
Sweet pepper, chilli pepper, cayenne

Half-hardy; must be kept free from frost

Family *Solanaceae*

Annual/perennial

Height: 30cm–2m (1–7ft)

Soil: any

Situation: hot, sunny

Propagation: seed

Main constituents: capsaicin, carotenoids, flavenoids, Vitamins A and C

Cultivation

There are two kinds of capsicum: *C. annuum,* which is an annual and called sweet pepper, and *C. frutescens,* a perennial, which is the chilli pepper family. I have put them together because their cultivation is very similar, as are many of their uses and properties.

The seeds need to germinate in warm soil, so in colder climates they are best sown in a heated propagator or greenhouse. Prick out into pots and then either plant outside or, in northern climates, plant in a greenhouse or in cold frames, especially if you wish the fruits to turn red. The perennial *C. frutescens* must be overwintered in a place where there is no danger of frost. *C. annuum* grows short and with large, bushy leaves, while the chilli plant can eventually grow quite tall with

Sweet pepper seedlings.

Sweet peppers can be grown in containers. This one is 'Redskin'. Note how the leaves turned towards the light. (I photographed it from behind, where the fruits were more visible.)

smaller leaves. Both have small white flowers, resembling potato flowers (they belong to the same family) and then bear green fruits which eventually turn red.

Chilli peppers growing in a greenhouse.

Other varieties

There are numerous varieties of both plants requiring the same cultivation. The main thing to remember is the smaller the fruit, the more pungent and fiery the taste.

Thus with *C. annuum* you can get varieties that produce very large red fruits (such as 'Redskin') which are sweet and mild, whereas varieties such as 'Hungarian Hot Wax' are

Sweet peppers in pots in a greenhouse. The variety is 'Hungarian Hot Wax'.

about half the size with a much more pungent flavour. Similarly, the larger, round C. *frutescens* such as 'Cherry' are relatively mild in comparison with 'Serrano'.

There are many modern varieties that produce different coloured fruits – yellow, orange or even purple – but I find their flavour somewhat inferior, although they do add variety of colour to many dishes.

Pests and diseases

If subjected to extremes of temperature or lack of ventilation, they can get fungal diseases or attacks of whitefly (see pages 56–7), so manage them carefully and do not use cold water. Slugs and leatherjackets have a taste for the small plants, especially the sweet peppers, so protect them or do not plant them out until they are large enough to withstand attack. Small aphids also tend to attack seedlings (the leaves become distorted) but the plants usually tend to 'grow out' of them.

History

The name comes from the Greek *kapto*, meaning to bite.

Both species come from tropical America and were first used by the Aztecs. Christopher Columbus brought the first capsicums back from the New World, and the species rapidly spread to Asia, Europe, and eventually to Hungary, where they are extensively cultivated (hence the name 'paprika'). C. *frutescens* is one of the main ingredients of all Indian and Eastern dishes.

Preserving and main uses

The fruits of both species can be used fresh: the mild varieties in

An unusual round variety of chilli pepper: 'Red Cherry'.

A variety of chilli pepper growing almost wild in an Asian garden.

Really hot chillis on sale in an Asian market.

salads and the fiery ones in stews and curries. They can be dried (see p. 62) and either used whole or ground into powder. Ground C. *annuum* becomes the 'Hungarian paprika' sold in the shops and C. *frutescens* becomes cayenne and forms the basis of Tabasco sauce and chilli powder.

The latter usually has other herbs mixed with it – cumin, garlic or oregano – and is therefore not quite as strong as pure cayenne. It is

worth remembering that if you use the seeds of either species, fresh or ground, the flavour gets 'hotter'.

Be careful when handling the seeds and wash your hands well if you are handling them without gloves. If you put your hands to your face, chilli can cause irritation and very sore eyes. Also, if you mistakenly eat a piece of chilli, gulping down water will not help – try a teaspoon of sugar!

Carum carvi
Caraway

Can be grown anywhere

Family *Umbelliferae*

Biennial

Height: up to 80cm (30in)

Soil: any

Situation: sunny

Propagation: seed

Main constituents: calcium, fixed oil, oxalate, proteins, volatile oils, resin

Cultivation

Seeds are best sown directly into the ground in spring. If you have a problem with slugs and the like, they can be raised in pots or boxes and transplanted but this is not always successful.

Caraway seems to tolerate almost any soil, but likes sun, especially in the second year, when the seeds ripen. Keep well weeded. The seeds should be harvested as soon as they darken. If you leave some seeds on one or two plants, they will self-seed and often small plants will come up in the autumn for harvesting the following year. To ensure a really good crop, though, sow each year in spring.

History

Evidence of the use of caraway goes back to the Stone Age. It is mentioned in the Bible, and the Ancient Egyptians and Arabs used it extensively, calling it Karawya.

In Shakespeare's *Henry IV*, Falstaff is invited by Squire Fallow to 'a pippin and a dish of caraways', while the seventeenth-century herbalist Parkinson wrote, 'the roots of caraway, being boiled, may be

Caraway plants in flower.
Inset shows seed heads ready for harvesting.

eaten as Carrots and by reason of the spice taste doth warme and comfort a cold and weak stomache, helping to dissolve Wind and to provoke Urine, and is a very welcome and delightful Dish to many'.

Caraway leaf.

Caraway seeds.

Preserving and main uses

When the seeds have darkened, hang up in bundles above a tray or container and as they dry thresh them. Store seeds in airtight jars.

They can be used in bread and vegetable dishes and with meat and cheese. In Germany, they make a liqueur from the seeds, *Kümmel*.

Young leaves can also be used and, in earlier times, the roots were prepared and eaten much like carrots or parsnips.

Cinnamomum verum
Cinnamon

Tropical tree/shrub requiring constant high temperature and humidity – not to be attempted in cold climates without an adequate greenhouse.

Family *Lauraceae*

Height: 6–9m (20–30ft)

Soil: rich, moist, well-drained and with plenty of sand

Situation: sun or part shade

Propagation: self-seeding in the wild, cuttings

Main constituents: volatile oil, tannins, mucilage, gum, sugar, resins, calcium, oxylate, coumarin

Cultivation

Space is not usually a problem for growing cinnamon trees, but maintaining a constant high temperature and humidity could be difficult unless you live in the tropics. If you intend growing cinnamon trees in a greenhouse, it is probably best to obtain an existing plant or some cuttings. These must be planted in humus-rich sandy soil. Keep humidity medium to high and never allow the soil to dry out (always use warm water); the temperature should not drop below 10°C (50°F). The ideal temperature is 16–33°C (61–91°F). Once the main stem reaches 1–2m (3–6ft) you can trim off the top and allow the wood to thicken. After three to five years the main stem should be ready for harvesting. Scrape off the bark with a very sharp knife and dry it. Then cut back the main stem and allow side shoots to develop which can in turn be harvested.

All the parts – leaves, flowers and bark – have the lovely cinnamon aroma, but only the bark is used in cooking.

History

Cinnamon trees are natives of Sri Lanka and the Moluccan Islands but are now widely grown throughout the tropics.

For centuries Arab and Chinese traders sold cinnamon to Europeans, who prized it highly, but were unable to discover its source until the early sixteenth century, when the Portuguese, Antonio de Abreu, and some Malay sailors set sail from Malacca, and discovered the Banda Islands in the Moluccas.

For nearly a hundred years the Europeans fought for supremacy of these islands, which eventually went to the VOC. The history of this and other spices is bloody and violent, and not infrequently the natives were massacred if they did not cooperate with the Dutch.

An Indonesian scraping off the bark from a cinnamon tree.

Other varieties

C. cassia is similar to *C. verum* and requires the same cultivation, but is generally considered to have an inferior flavour.

Pests and diseases

In the wild, cinnamon trees suffer from few pests but in glasshouse conditions beware of the usual pests (see pages 56–7).

Preserving and main uses

The bark should be dried in hot sunlight and stored in airtight jars. Westerners use cinnamon, whole or ground, mainly to flavour fruit and cakes, but Asians employ it in many savoury dishes and make delicious tea from it.

Cinnamon sticks and powdered cinnamon.

A piece of fresh cinnamon bark.

Cinnamon trees.

oriandrum sativum
Coriander, dizzycorn, Chinese parsley

Can be grown anywhere

Family *Umbelliferae*
Annual
Height: 30–60cm (1–2ft)
Soil: any
Situation: sunny
Propagation: seed
Main constituents: volatile oil

Cultivation
Sow seeds directly into the ground as the seedlings do not like to be transplanted. If you are an avid user of the leaves, make a succession of sowings so you have a constant supply. Coriander will not grow in winter in cold climates, but in warm regions you can get leaves all the year round. If left to mature, the plants will produce delicate white or pink flowers and then the round seeds which are also extensively used in cooking.

If you want both the leaves and seeds, plan your sowings accordingly: leave an early sowing to mature in good time to harvest the seeds. Coriander will self-seed. In fact, one of my best crops came from plants I had left standing all autumn.

Pests and diseases
Seedlings are prone to slug and leatherjacket attacks but diseases are rare.

History
Coriander has been grown for thousands of years by both the Egyptians and the Ancient Greeks,

Coriander in flower.

who unflatteringly called it *Koris* (bug) because of the pungent smell of mature plants.

It is mentioned as an aphrodisiac in the Arabian tales of *A Thousand and One-Nights*, but it was the Romans who spread it throughout Europe as well as to the East, where it is now extensively used, especially in India.

Preserving and main uses
The leaves are best used fresh as they neither dry nor freeze well. Plants with seeds should be hung up to dry and the seeds shaken into a container. They can be used whole or, more commonly, ground. Leaves can be used in salads, sauces and Eastern dishes and the crushed seeds form part of garam masala and are widely used in curries.

Coriander seeds.

A single herb, such as coriander, growing in a small bed inset into brick paving can look very attractive.

Crocus sativus
Saffron

Can be grown anywhere

Family *Iridaceae*

Perennial

Height: 20–30cm (9–12in)

Soil: rich, well-drained

Situation: sunny and sheltered

Propagation: division of corms

Main constituents: crocin, essential oil

Cultivation

Saffron should be grown the same way as its close relative the spring crocus, which it resembles. Were it not for the fact that it flowers in autumn, it could easily be mistaken for the common crocus. It is best to buy bulbs, which should be planted about 8cm (3in) apart in a well-sheltered sunny position in late summer, where they will flower the same year. Once established in a position they like, they will flower every autumn and need little attention except for weeding and dividing the corms every two or three years.

Other varieties

C. sativus flowers only in autumn (either purple or white flowers) but should not be confused with other species of autumn crocus, especially *Colchicum* spp. (known as autumn crocus or meadow saffron), which are poisonous.

Autumn crocuses – poisonous.

History

The origins of *C. sativus* are obscure but it is an ancient spice, cultivated by the Minoans, the Ancient Greeks and the Romans.

Apparently Romans who wanted to stay reasonably sober at a party took a good dose of saffron water

A painting in Knossos c. 1500BC, showing a monkey trained to gather saffron flowers.

beforehand. It was brought to Northern Europe by the Romans but then disappeared until the Crusaders reintroduced it. It was extensively grown in Saffron Walden (hence the name) in England until the harvesting became too expensive. The town's shield still bears three saffron flowers. Nowadays large crops are grown in Nepal.

Preserving and main uses

Saffron is one of the most expensive of all spices. Even today it can only be harvested by hand, and it takes about 150,000 flowers to produce 1kg (2lb) of saffron. Flowers should be picked when fully open, preferably in the morning, and the stigma and style pinched out and dried in a dark place. It is used extensively the world over to flavour and colour rice and other dishes, especially paellas, bouillabaisses and risottos, as well as cakes and bread. It should not be confused with turmeric powder, which also colours rice and other dishes. In Asia, turmeric is sometimes sold as saffron, but their flavours are quite different.

Pinch out stigma and style when flower is fully open.

Saffron strands.

Cuminum cyminum
Cumin

Requires protection from frost

Family *Umbelliferae*

Annual

Height: 15cm (6in)

Soil: well-drained and rich

Situation: sunny

Propagation: seed

Main constituents: volatile oil

Cultivation

In tropical climates, cumin is easily grown outside and seed can be sown directly into the ground. Where the climate is cold or only temperate, it is best to grow cumin in a greenhouse. It likes lots of sun and good rich soil. If your summers are hot and your winters cold, you can sow seed in a heated greenhouse or propagator and then plant the seedlings out very carefully (try not to disturb the roots) as they do not much like being transplanted.

History

Cumin is indigenous to Egypt but is now grown all over the world, especially in the East, where it is used extensively. Isaiah mentions it in the Old Testament and Matthew again in the New, reinforcing the influence herbs and spices have exerted on history: 'Woe unto you, scribes and Pharisees, hypocrites! for ye tithe mint and anise and cummin, and have left undone the weightier matters of the law, judgment and mercy, and faith' (Matthew xxiii.23).

The Celts baked fish with cumin and it was a common plant in medieval herb gardens, but later it seems to have fallen out of favour in the West, having been more or less replaced after the seventeenth century by caraway. It is now enjoying a comeback, doubtless due to the popularity of curries and Eastern dishes.

Other varieties

Although all cumins look the same, there are varieties that vary in strength, such as black cumin (*C. nigrum*), which has a more delicate flavour. There is, however, usually only one variety of seed sold in Western shops.

Preserving and main uses

Cumin should be harvested in exactly the same way as its numerous cousins, whom it also resembles: caraway, anise, dill and indeed all the seed-bearing *Umbelliferae* herbs and spices.

Hang bunches in a dry place and, when dry, thresh them and store seeds in airtight jars.

Seeds can be ground or used whole in an enormous variety of dishes: meat, chicken, fish, curries, stews, bread and cakes.

If you are using seeds whole, they should first be lightly fried and then cooked in order to obtain the best flavour.

Cumin is one of the five ground spices of the panchphoran spice mix which is frequently encountered in Bengal, and it is also used in Mexican cooking.

Panchphoran consists of cumin, fennel, fenugreek, and *Nigella* seeds (the latter are not in this book) as well as *radhuni* seeds. These are only available in Bengal, but you could use black mustard seeds instead.

Young cumin plant growing in a greenhouse border.

Curcuma domestica
Turmeric, Indian saffron

Tropical plant requiring heated greenhouse and medium/high humidity when grown in temperate climates

Family *Zingiberaceae*

Perennial

Height: 1m (3ft)

Soil: rich, well-drained

Situation: very warm but not direct sun

Propagation: rhizomes

Main constituents: albumen, curcumin, potassium, Vitamin C, volatile oil.

Cultivation

Although a native of the tropics, turmeric can be grown quite easily in temperate countries in a heated greenhouse or a similar warm, light place where the temperature does not drop below 12°C (54°F) in winter and 15°C (59°F) in summer. I have grown it from pieces of fresh turmeric bought in a supermarket.

Turmeric growing indoors in a pot.

Turmeric growing wild in Asia.

Use a rich mixture of soil, compost and humus but make sure it drains really well. It grows in tropical rainforest areas where the soil is covered by inches of humus and, despite rain, drains quickly.

Make sure that the pieces you use (they can be quite small) have 'eyes' and plant them about 5–10cm (2–4in) deep. Water regularly (being careful not to use cold water), and keep as humid as possible. In a few weeks it will have developed long stately leaves (not unlike those of banana plants), and eventually it produces a flower at the centre.

It makes an elegant pot plant, but will not produce any seeds.

Pests and diseases

If grown indoors, watch out for greenhouse pests such as red spider mite and scale insect (see pp. 56–7).

Turmeric in flower. This happens rarely, and fruits are not produced.

History

Although turmeric is grown all over the tropics and is widely used as a dye, and in curries and other dishes, virtually no folklore seems to exist. In Thailand they use it to dye the robes of Buddhist monks and in India it is one of the main constituents in curries.

It certainly came to Europe in the Middle Ages, when it was called Indian or Eastern saffron, but neither Culpeper nor Gerard makes any mention of it.

Preserving and main uses

Once the rhizomes have matured (after about twelve months), boil, peel and dry them and then grind them to a powder. Store in a dark place.

Turmeric is mainly used in curries, but it is also used in liqueurs and cheeses.

Turmeric as sold in Eastern markets.

19

Elettaria cardamomum
Cardamom

Tropical plant requiring heated greenhouse when grown in cold climates

Family *Zingiberaceae*

Perennial

Height: 3m (9ft)

Soil: rich in compost and humus

Situation: hot, but some shade

Propagation: seed, division or cuttings

Main constituents: cineol, gum, starch, volatile oil

Cultivation

If grown from seed, a cardamom plant will take three to five years to mature, but a stem cutting will only take about one to three years. In cold climates, it can be grown in pots or greenhouses providing the temperature is kept around 22°C (72°F) and the roots are never allowed to dry out. The many leaf stems grow up to 3m (9ft) high, and, as it is evergreen, cardamom can make an attractive bushy pot plant.

If grown outside its natural environment in a greenhouse or pot, you may have a problem in getting it to produce flower stems. These are much shorter than the leaf stems, and grow horizontally near the ground. They will bear a succession of whitish flowers with a bluish tip that turn into the seed-bearing pods. This is a continuous process over several months and each pod must be picked individually when not yet completely ripe.

Pests and diseases

Cardamoms are prone to mosaic viruses and some insect damage. My own indoor plants have suffered from several attacks of scale insect. If these are spotted in time, they can easily be kept under control by wiping them off manually. Watch carefully for any signs, especially at the back of fresh, young leaves.

History

Cardamom grows wild in many parts of Asia, but the true cardamom grows in south-western India and Sri Lanka, at heights of around 1,000m (3,500ft).

It was used by Orientals at least 1,000 years BC but was not brought to Europe until about the fourth century by the Ancient Greeks and Romans. The latter, especially, used it in cooking and as a cure for stomach aches. The Arabs mix it, even today, with coffee beans to make their own distinctive coffee brew.

Preserving and main uses

The green pods should be washed and then dried, either in the sun or in a very warm room. In the sun, the pods turn white, but they remain green if dried away from the sun. Each pod contains up to twenty seeds. Do not take out the seeds until you actually want to use them.

They can be used (whole or ground into powder) in curries and Eastern dishes. In Europe, especially in Scandinavia, they are used to flavour cakes and pastries.

Seed pods are green as they have been dried away from sunlight.

Young cardamom growing indoors in a pot.

Foeniculum vulgare
Fennel

Can be grown anywhere

Family *Umbelliferae*

Hardy perennial

Height: up to 2m (7ft)

Soil: any, well-drained

Situation: sunny

Propagation: seed, division

Main constituents: flavonoids, fixed oil, minerals, vitamins, volatile oil

Cultivation

Sow seeds in spring directly in the ground or in boxes and transplant. Fennel is easy to grow as it is not fussy about soil and seems not to be troubled by any pests, but it does like sun. Some people say that other plants do not like fennel and therefore it should be kept well away from other crops, especially beans. I have not tested this theory, but mine grows alongside other tall plants and they seem to cohabit quite peacefully. Do not, however, grow fennel with similar *Umbelliferae* such as dill and allow them to self-seed, as the two will probably cross-pollinate and you may get some strange hybrids.

Fennel will readily seed itself, and you can also divide the roots of older plants.

Other varieties

There is a bronze variety (see page 59) of *F. vulgare* which makes a handsome plant, and also *F. v.* var. *dulce*. The latter is an annual and really a vegetable – the bulbous root is the part that is eaten.

Fennel grows really tall. Some of these seed heads are ready for harvesting.

History

Fennel is a native of Mediterranean countries but has been grown for centuries all over the world. It was always said to possess countless powers: the Chinese and Hindus used it against snakebite; the ancient Greeks and Romans considered it a symbol of power and success, and also an aid to good eyesight and a means of increasing a mother's milk; in medieval times it warded off witches, bad breath and obesity. Indeed, it was good for a myriad of ailments as well as for all kinds of culinary dishes. It was the main ingredient of gripe water to help babies' wind. Today, some babies are still given mild fennel tea.

Preserving and main uses

The leaves are best fresh but can be frozen. Use in salads, soups, stews and fish dishes. Harvest the seeds when they begin to turn brown, hang to dry and store in airtight jars. The seeds can be used in bread and cakes as well as sauces and other dishes. The stems can be dried and used like the leaves.

Fennel.

Hyssopus officinalis
Hyssop

Can be grown anywhere

Family *Labiatae*

Hardy perennial

Height: 50cm (20in)

Soil: any

Situation: sunny or part shade, dry

Propagation: seed, cuttings or division

Main constituents: flavonoids, gum, hyssopin, marrubiin, resin, tannin, volatile oil

Cultivation

Hyssop is a slow grower but once established it is very hardy and will keep going for years. In warm climates, seeds can be sown direct into the ground, but in most cases it is best to start them indoors at a temperature of not less than 21°C (70°F). Alternatively, buy one or two plants and then take cuttings in autumn (in very sandy soil) or divide existing plants in spring.

Hyssop is a handsome plant and can be grown as a small hedge. Its flowers can be pink, white or blue. The latter is the true variety and the most robust. Cut right back in autumn (to encourage soft green stems and leaves) and feed liberally each year.

It is said to protect brassicas from the cabbage butterfly. It is certainly loved by many species of butterfly.

Other varieties

H. o. 'Aristatus' (rock hyssop) – a short compact variety the leaves of which have similar properties.

All varieties make good pot plants.

Rock hyssop is a robust, compact plant which makes a good border or a small hedge.

History

Hyssop is an ancient herb, a native of Europe and Asia. There are numerous references to it in the Bible. David in Psalm 51 prays 'purge me with hyssop and I shall be clean'. It is also referred to at the Crucifixion.

The name comes from the Hebrew word *azob* (holy herb), and hyssop was formerly often used in consecrating churches.

Many ancient tribal rituals, so often disregarded by scientists of the nineteenth and early twentieth centuries, are now being proved to have been correct all along. In the case of hyssop, research shows that the mould that produces penicillin grows on the plant, and it therefore has many anti-viral properties. This fact was unknown centuries ago when, nevertheless, they bathed lepers in hyssop.

Preserving and main uses

Use sparingly in cooking as the marrubiin it contains gives it a bitter flavour.

It is good in stuffings, salads and with some fruit, and is especially good with oily fish and fatty meats. Both leaves and flowers can be dried, but avoid the woody stems.

*J*uniperus communis
Juniper

Can be grown anywhere

Juniperus communis.

Family *Cupressaceae*

Hardy tree

Height: 6m (20ft)

Soil: any

Situation: any

Propagation: seed and cuttings

Main constituents: flavonoids, gallotannins, resin, sugars, Vitamin C, volatile oil

Cultivation

When growing junipers the main requirement is patience! Junipers need separate male and female plants in order to produce their aromatic berries. So start by buying two small plants, one of each gender (make sure the nursery does sell you one of each as they are similar in appearance and can only be told apart by the presence of fruit or flowers). Alternatively, get cuttings of both male and female trees. The flowers of the male trees are yellow and the female green.

Cuttings (15–20cm (6–8in) long) of the current year's ripened growth should be put in pots or direct into the ground in autumn. Strip off needles 2–3cm (1–2in) from the butt and plant approx 10cm (4in) deep. Transplant to their final position once well rooted.

Junipers are very hardy; they will tolerate wind, sun and snow and both acid and alkaline soils. The berries, which are formed by female flowers, appear after several years, but will take two to three years to ripen from green to dark blue. If you are really ambitious to grow everything from seed, sow them in

autumn and be prepared for a long wait – often they will take two or three years to germinate and then it will be several more years before they bear fruit!

Other varieties

There are a great many varieties of *J. communis,* including the Irish juniper 'Hibernica', which grows in a narrow pointed column, and *J. c.* 'Depressa aurea', which is short and golden and ideal for ground cover. There are also Chinese, Californian and Pfitzer varieties.

History

J. communis is probably a native of Northern Europe, but it seems to have grown for centuries both in the hot climates of Asia and right up to the Arctic Circle. It was once used to ward off evil spirits, devils and wild animals, no doubt due to the fact is was mentioned in the Bible as a protective plant.

At one time none-too-honest traders in rare spices added the dark-blue/black berries to expensive black peppercorns (*Piper nigrum*; see p. 41). The delicate juniper berries would absorb the pungent pepper flavour and most customers would be none the wiser!

Preserving and main uses

Harvest the berries when they turn dark blue, then dry and store them. The berries are used to make gin and various spirits but in cooking they are wonderful in marinades, sauces and pâtés, especially of game and poultry.

They should not be eaten by people with kidney problems or pregnant women as they encourage uterine contractions.

Three years' berries on the same plant – green, blue and dark blue. The dark ones are ready to harvest.

Dried juniper berries.

Laurus nobilis
Bay, sweet bay, sweet laurel, noble bay

Can be grown anywhere but protect from extreme cold and wind

Family *Lauraceae*

Perennial evergreen

Height: 2–20m (7–70ft)

Soil: well-manured

Situation: sunny and sheltered from wind

Propagation: seed, cuttings and layering

Main constituents: tannic acid, volatile oil

Cultivation

Except in ideal conditions, when it can grow up to 20m (70ft), bay remains a small tree or shrub. Bay is rarely grown from seed. It is a frustrating pastime as the seeds often do not germinate even if sown in heat. It is better to take cuttings from mature growth and plant them in pots or boxes. Keep in a cool greenhouse or cover with inflated plastic bags. Harden off in the sun and plant out in about six months. Bay can also be layered.

Be sure to plant in a spot well sheltered from winds, or, better still, keep it in a tub or pot which can be brought indoors in cold, windy weather. You can prune the plant into almost any shape.

Other varieties

L. nobilis aurea has golden leaves and *L. nobilis angustifolia* has much narrower leaves.

Pests and diseases

If grown indoors, beware of scale insects.

History

Bay was used by the Greeks and Romans to make the laurel crowns awarded to victorious athletes and warriors, and great artists and writers. The modern academic Bachelor of Arts comes from bay – baccalaureate: the French *bachelier* (bachelor) and laurel.

Culpeper writes, 'it is a tree of the sun, and under the celestial sign Leo, and resisteth witchcraft very potently, as also all the evils old Saturn can do to the body of man . . .'.

Preserving and main uses

Use fresh, or dry the leaves in a dark place. The fresh leaves are much stronger than the dried. Bay is an essential part of the bouquet garni and can be used in almost all savoury dishes. It can also be used in milk to flavour puddings and custards.

Bay tree in flower.

A small potted bay tree in plenty of mulch overwintering in a greenhouse. Note the bubble plastic on inside of glass.

Bay leaves.

evisticum officinale
Lovage, Old English lovage, Cornish lovage

Can be grown anywhere

Family *Umbelliferae*

Hardy perennial

Height: 2m (7ft)

Soil: any

Situation: any

Propagation: seed, division of roots

Main constituents: acids, courmarins, gum, resin, volatile oil

Cultivation

One or two plants will probably serve most families' needs. Either buy a small plant or sow seeds in spring or late summer. Lovage will grow almost anywhere but as it is tall and vigorous, choose its permanent position carefully. It will readily self-seed.

Divide roots every few years, or allow self-seeded plants to grow and dig up old ones.

History

Lovage is a native of the Balkans but was spread round Europe by the Romans. It was used as a panacea for almost any ailment: those of the stomach, eyes, and ears; infections, spots, freckles, and even pleurisy. Culpeper, too, lists a host of cures including that 'it openeth, cureth and digesteth humours, and mightily provoketh women's courses and urine'.

This well-established plant requires division.

Preserving and main uses

The leaves, flowers, seeds, stems and roots can all be used. Dry or freeze the leaves, and dry the seeds and roots.

The leaves can be used in salads, stock and stews; seeds can be used in bread and pastries or added to drinks; and the stems can be eaten raw, used in stews, sauces, or soups, or crystallised. The roots are mainly used medicinally, but can be peeled and cooked.

Do not keep dried parts for more than a year, and experiment with the use of lovage cautiously as it has a very distinctive strong flavour.

Lovage leaves.

Lovage seeds.

Lovage makes a stunning leafy plant in the early part of its growth.

ippia citriodora
syn. Aloysia triphylla

Lemon verbena, herb Louise

Tender shrub requiring protection from frost

Family *Verbenaceae*

Half-hardy perennial shrub

Height: up to 5m (16ft)

Soil: any, but rich in compost

Situation: sunny (part shade in greenhouse)

Propagation: seed if available; cuttings

Main constituents: essential oil

Cultivation

Buy one or two plants (or take some cuttings from a friend's) and plant them in summer. Seeds, if you can get them, can be sown in spring, but germination is very erratic and can be very frustrating.

Lemon verbena growing in an unheated greenhouse.

A mass of lemon verbena growing outside in Australia.

Lemon verbena must be protected from frost, so either grow it in a frost-free position outside, or, in chilly climates, establish a plant in a greenhouse or conservatory, where it will grow to at least 1 or 2m (3–7ft).

Alternatively, bring the plant indoors in winter. If grown outside, poor soil will make the plant hardier, but it will not develop the long, lush, graceful branches that are typical of this plant. I have just one plant in an unheated greenhouse, which has to be cut back quite severely each year as otherwise it would take over.

Pests and diseases

If grown in a greenhouse, watch out for whitefly (see pp. 56-57). An attack of this pest will not kill an established plant, but it could be disastrous for small plants and cuttings.

History

Lemon verbena is a native of South America and was brought to Europe by the Spaniards in the seventeenth century. It grows mainly in Chile and Peru, where it reaches a height of 5m (16ft) or more. The Spaniards grow it for its perfumed oil, and it was also used medicinally in Europe, mainly against stomach complaints.

Surprisingly, there is little else known about the plant, which is now becoming popular due to its wonderful lemon scent.

Preserving and main uses

Only use the leaves, preferably fresh. They can be dried or frozen into ice-cubes and used in drinks. Use in stuffings, preserves and desserts, and (sparingly) in fish dishes.

Lemon verbena leaves.

Melissa officinalis
Lemon balm, bee balm, melissa, sweet balm

Can be grown anywhere

Family *Labiatae*

Hardy perennial

Height: 1m (3ft)

Soil: any

Situation: part shade

Propagation: seed division or cuttings

Main constituents: flavonoids, tannin, volatile oil

Cultivation

Although slow to germinate from seed, lemon balm can be very invasive once established. Not only does it readily seed itself, but it also spreads along the ground like a creeping buttercup. If left unchecked, it will take over. It makes a good pot plant, so either keep it in check that way, or sink some boards into the ground to prevent it spreading too far.

If sowing seeds, do not cover them but just press them lightly into the soil. Thin out and transplant as soon as large enough to handle. Personally, I find one or two plants quite sufficient for one household.

Propagate also by root division almost any time, but preferably in spring or autumn. You can also strike cuttings from mature shoots. Keep moist.

Lemon balm is one of the easiest and most trouble-free herbs.

Other varieties

There is a smaller variety with mottled yellow leaves *(M. o. variegata)* which grows only about 30cm (12in) tall and which makes a good pot plant.

Variegated lemon balm.

History

A native of Europe, lemon balm was used by the Ancient Greeks and subsequently throughout Europe, largely as a medicinal herb. A host of health-giving properties were attributed to it, some of which science is now proving to have been correct. It was said to cure bites and wounds (it certainly has a good effect on them), as well as 'strengthening the brain' and memory, and driving away melancholy, preventing baldness. It was also said to be 'useful against headaches and neuralgic affections'.

Melissa is Greek for bee. Bees certainly love this plant and some people have grown quantities of balm in orchards to attract bees for pollinating blossom.

Preserving and main uses

Only the leaves are used; they should be harvested just before the plant flowers, when their flavour is at its best. Leaves can be dried, but will then lose much of their flavour.

Use in drinks, fish, meat and poultry dishes as well as sauces and custards and with fruit.

Common lemon balm.

Lemon balm leaves.

M entha spicata
syn. M. viridis

Mint

Can be grown anywhere

Mentha aquatica.

Family *Labiatae*

Perennial

Height: 30cm (1ft)

Soil: rich in compost

Situation: any

Propagation: seed, division of roots, cuttings

Main constituents: flavonoids, rosmaric acid, tannin, volatile oil

Cultivation

There are endless varieties of mint, most of them very easy to grow, but the one most commonly grown for cooking is the wild variety *M. spicata* (spearmint).

All mints grow rapidly in all directions and need therefore to be contained. I find that bottomless buckets or large pots make good 'restrictors'.

Wooden boards sunk into the ground help, but healthy mints will probably find their way over or under them.

Sow seeds in spring directly into the ground, or, better still, get some root cuttings – one or two will suffice as they take easily – and keep them moist, feed with compost and you will have mint for many, many years.

If you grow several varieties of mint, they will probably hybridise and you could well get your own species of mint.

Mentha gentilis.

Other varieties

There are over one hundred varieties of mint. Here are just a few:

M. aquatica (water mint). A good variety if you have a stream or watery plot.

M. gentilis. Spicy scent.

M. piperita (peppermint). Grows up to 1m (3 ft).

M. citrata (Eau de Cologne mint). Sharp lemon scent.

M. pulegium (pennyroyal). Prostrate peppermint-scented. Likes damp shade.

M. rotundifolia variegata. A pretty variety with a pineapple scent.

M. suaveolens crispii. Smaller with curly leaves and apple-scented.

M. requienii (Corsican mint). Small mint only 2–3cm (1in) tall. This variety will decoratively creep over stones and walls. It will also make a herb lawn which is wonderful to walk over.

M. suaveolens (applemint). Apple-scented.

Do not grow different varieties in close proximity as the stronger varieties will swamp the less vigorous ones.

Mentha spicata.

Pineapple mint (Mentha rotundifolia variegata)

Mentha citrata.

Pests and diseases

Slugs and some varieties of small caterpillar occasionally attack mint. Mints are said to be good companion plants for brassicas as they deter cabbage butterflies, but I have never tested this theory. Mice are also said to be averse to the smell of mints. Mints can also suffer from a fungus, mint rust; the leaves become contorted and then orange-spotted. Do not try to cure it with fungal sprays, but simply dig up unaffected roots and replant elsewhere. Burn affected plants and roots and do not plant mints in that spot for several years.

Mentha requieni grown as a pot plant.

History

The word *mentha* came from a legend in Greek mythology which recounts that Pluto, god of the underworld, became infatuated with a beautiful nymph, Menthe. His enraged wife, Persephone, cursed her and turned her into a herb destined to grow forever in moist shady places.

The origins of mint seem obscure; different varieties probably grew the world over. The Chinese and the Indians have long used mint and evidence of its use by the Mycenaean civilisation has been found.

In the Bible the Pharisees imposed taxes on mint (see page 18). The reported powers and uses of mint were even more legion than the varieties – it was said to cure dozens of ailments, was used for potpourris, sachets and fragrant baths, sweets and chewing gum; it soothed wasp stings and the bites of mad dogs . . . and all this quite apart from its many culinary uses.

Preserving and main uses

Use fresh leaves whenever possible, but they can also be dried or deep frozen. Hang the leaves in bunches to dry and store in airtight jars in a dark place.

Use in sauces with meat (especially lamb) and with vegetables, fruit and drinks. Eastern recipes and curries also use mints.

Mentha suaveolens.

Peppermint leaves.

M onarda didyma
Bergamot, bee balm, Indian plume, Oswego tea

Can be grown anywhere

Family *Labiatae*

Hardy perennial

Height: 30–100cm (1–3ft)

Soil: light, moist

Situation: part shade

Propagation: seeds, root division, cuttings

Main constituents: tannic acid, volatile oil (comprising thymol)

Cultivation

Either sow seeds in spring or take cuttings from an existing plant. Cuttings will strike easily either in plain water or sand. Thin or transplant to about 45cm (18in) apart. Bergamot likes moisture, so take care that the ground does not dry out, as plants will become weak and straggly.

Clumps should be divided every three or four years. Rosemary and bergamot look attractive together and can be made into a small hedge. (Plant the bergamot behind the rosemary.)

Bergamot is an excellent plant for bees.

Other varieties

There is a wild variety, *M. fistulosa*, which is strongly scented, with lavender-coloured flowers. There is also a tender annual variety, *M. citriodora*, with unusual pink flowers which, when dried, are used for decoration. The leaves are used for tea.

History

Bergamot comes from North America, where the Oswego Indians (hence the name) used it to cure almost anything from wounds, indigestion and abscesses to bronchial problems and hair lotions. The thymol that the plant contains is highly antiseptic.

It became a popular tea substitute after the Boston Tea Party (1773) and was introduced to Europe when settlers sent back seed. The name comes from that of the Spanish botanist Dr Nicholas Monardes, who wrote a herbal of North American plants in 1569.

Preserving and main uses

Dry the leaves and flowers. Leaves can also be frozen in ice cubes and used to flavour drinks, while the fresh flowers are a pretty addition to salads and drinks. Use leaves (sparingly) in stuffings and with meat.

The main use of bergamot is flavouring drinks and making teas.

Monarda didyma.

Bergamot leaves.

Myrrhis odorata

Sweet cicely, sweet chervil, anise fern, great chervil, cow chervil

Can be grown anywhere

Family *Umbelliferae*

Hardy perennial

Height: 1–1.5m (3–5ft)

Soil: rich, moist

Situation: part shade

Propagation: seed, division

Main constituents: glycyrrhizin

Cultivation

Sweet cicely is a tall, pretty, fern-like plant that likes shade, moisture and lots of humus.

Sow the long brown glossy seeds in autumn; they require cold temperatures before germinating in the warming soil in spring. Alternatively, keep the seeds in your refrigerator for several weeks and then sow in spring. Plant about

Sweet cicely eventually grows into a large but dainty plant.

Ripe sweet-cicely seeds ready for harvesting.

60cm (2ft) apart. If you want to use the seeds, allow the plant to flower and harvest some seeds whilst they are still green. Sweet cicely will happily self-seed.

When plants get large, divide them. Sweet cicely is a good plant for bees.

Other varieties

A plant from North America which looks very much the same and has similar uses is *Osmorhiza longistylis*.

Pests and diseases

Watch out for fungal diseases. Cut off the affected parts and burn them.

History

Sweet cicely is actually a native of Great Britain, but it is now found in hilly, moist places just about anywhere.

It has been used as a medicinal and culinary herb for centuries, but there is little magic or legend attached to it. It has been described as 'so harmless you cannot use it amiss'.

The leaves, seeds and roots are all used, and Culpeper says: 'They are all three of them of the nature of Jupiter, and under his dominion. This whole plant, besides its pleasantness in salads, hath its physical virtue. The root, boiled and eaten with oil and vinegar (or without oil), do much please and warm old and cold stomachs oppressed with wind or phlegm . . .'.

Preserving and main uses

Use fresh leaves in salads, stews, soups and with vegetables; they do not dry well. You can use green seeds in fruit salads and ice cream and ripe seeds in cooked dishes such as apple pie.

The peeled roots can be either eaten raw or cooked.

The fern-like leaves are useful for decorating salads and add a faint aniseed flavour.

Myristica fragrans
Nutmeg, mace

Tropical tree: if grown in cold climates requires large heated and humid greenhouse

Nutmeg trees in the same plantation as photo on left.

Family *Myristicaceae*

Tender evergreen tree

Height: up to 7m (23ft)

Soil: rich; full of humus

Situation: hot and humid with some shade

Propagation: seed or cuttings

Main constituents: acids, volatile oil

Cultivation

The nutmeg is a bushy tree which can grow to 7m (23ft) or more. Unless you have a very large heated and humid greenhouse or conservatory and lots of patience, do not attempt to grow it. The temperature should not fall below 16°C (61°F), and ideally should be maintained at 24–33°C (75–91°F).

Nutmeg is a fascinating spice and one which has caused much strife in its history. It will give you immense satisfaction if you grow it.

To obtain a crop you will need both a male and female tree. The seeds (or nuts) take about six weeks to germinate, during which time the temperature must be kept around 25–30°C (77–86°F) minimum and constantly humid.

The seedlings grow very slowly and it will be seven years before you can obtain a crop. The fruit, when it develops, is like a large plum, and when ripe, the flesh bursts to reveal its secrets: a lobed crimson covering around the nut which is called an aril and which, when dried, becomes the mace sold in shops. Inside the aril is a nut which, when shelled, becomes the familiar nutmeg.

Only harvest fruits that are beginning to burst. A good tree will produce nutmegs all the year. If you pick all the fruits at one time, ripe and unripe, you will eventually make the plant sterile.

In the tropics, nutmegs need some shade from the fierce sun. This plantation has huge, magnificent almond trees scattered throughout. They tower above the nutmegs and provide the necessary shade.

Unripe nutmeg fruits.

History

Nutmeg trees are now widely grown in tropical areas, but they originated in the group of Indonesian islands called the Moluccas and more specifically from the tiny group known as the Bandas (see page 15).

Somehow the Arabs brought the nutmeg to Europe as early as the sixth century, when it became a rare and much-sought-after spice. Chaucer said people liked to spice beer with nutmeg and often 0.5kg (1lb) cost as much as three sheep or a cow.

The Dutch, who eventually controlled the Moluccas, resorted to dubious practices to keep up the price, and vast plantations were burnt. At one point an ignorant bureaucrat in Amsterdam ordered the Moluccans to cut down their nutmeg trees and grow mace instead! By the eighteenth or nineteenth centuries, however, both the British and the French had contrived (independently) to obtain plants and took them to Mauritius, Ceylon and the West Indies.

Preserving and main uses

The mace (aril) should be dried in the sun and kept in airtight containers. Keep the nut in its shell as long as possible and then shell and grate it as you need it. Do not grind the nut to a powder, or it will soon lose its strong flavour.

Use both the nut and the mace sparingly in both sweet and savoury dishes, as well as with milk and cheese. Try grating nutmeg on to Brussels sprouts.

The outer plum-like flesh (covering the mace) can also be used to make jam. Mace is used extensively for pickles.

Split nutmeg fruits ready for harvesting showing red mace.

Mace drying in the sun.

Nutmegs without their shells.

Nutmegs drying in the sun.

33

O cimum basilicum
Basil, sweet basil

Requires protection from frost

Family *Labiatae*

Annual/perennial

Height: 30–60cm (1–2ft)

Soil: richly manured

Situation: sunny

Propagation: seed

Main constituents: camphor, essential oil, tannins

Cultivation

In its native India, basil can be grown and picked for many, many months and can, therefore, almost be called a perennial. However, wherever there are cold winds or danger of frost, basil must be treated as an annual.

It makes an excellent pot plant, so with enough warmth and light, you can have this wonderful herb fresh all the year. As soon as the soil has warmed up, sow seeds in pots or where they are to grow. For best results in cold climates, grow in a greenhouse border in front of tomatoes or melons. Basil dislikes being transplanted, but I have done so frequently with success as I wanted a large crop and space in my greenhouse was limited. Unless you

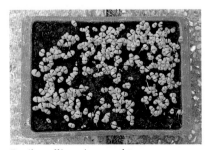

Basil seedlings in a seed tray.

Seedlings in pots: Left – sweet basil; right – bush basil.

want to collect your own seeds, pick leaves frequently: pinch out tops to encourage bushy growth.

Protect from scorching sun and water in the middle of the day and also spray leaves with water.

Other varieties

Personally, I think the ordinary *O. basilicum* has the best flavour for cooking, but there are several other decorative varieties all requiring similar cultivation.

O. b. purpurea (dark opal basil) makes quite a handsome pot plant, especially the 'ruffles' variety.

There is also *O. b. citriodorum*, which has lemon-scented leaves, while *O. b. minimum* (bush basil) has smaller leaves, is hardier than the others and will tolerate poor soil.

Pests and diseases

Slugs and similar pests seem to have a taste for basil seedlings (see pp. 56-57), which is why on the whole I prefer to grow them in small pots and transplant them outside when they are growing vigorously.

Basils are also susceptible to wilts and rust. If you find this is a problem, dig up the affected plants and burn them, or put them in a well-heated compost heap.

Careful management will prevent diseases; above all, do not overwater basil plants nor subject them to cold water.

History

Historically, basil seems to have a split personality. In the East, especially in India, it is revered; it is

Sweet basil.

Purple basil 'ruffles'.

grown in temples and placed on the dead to ward off evil. Indians also chose basil on which to swear oaths in court. European physicians and herbalists, on the other hand, regarded it as virulent and even poisonous and believed it fostered hate, misfortune and poverty. Another superstition was that the plants bred scorpions, and that even smelling it might bring a scorpion on to the brain.

Preserving and main uses

Nothing can compare with the flavour and aroma of fresh basil, but dry leaves as quickly as possible, away from the sun, and store in airtight jars; alternatively freeze. Whole plants (before flowers appear) can be pulled up and dried. Leaves can also be stored by packing them into jars of olive oil. Alternatively, put into crocks with alternate layers of leaves and coarse salt. Wash before use.

Basil can be used in a multitude of vegetable and meat dishes and sauces, and especially with pasta.

Mixed basils growing in pots in the greenhouse.

Basil leaves.

origanum majorana
Sweet marjoram, knotted marjoram

Some varieties require protection from frost

Family *Labiatae*

Perennial/annual

Height: 15–60cm (6in–2ft)

Soil: rich, slightly alkaline

Situation: sunny

Propagation: seed, division or cuttings

Main constituents: essential oil, resins, tannic acids

Cultivation

There is a lot of confusion about all the varieties of marjorams and origanums and, indeed, about which are which. All are used for culinary, medicinal and cosmetic purposes, but the one most used in cooking is the sweet marjoram.

The varieties below all require similar cultivation – they are, in fact, easier as they are hardier than *O. majorana* and once established will grow indefinitely. Although *O. majorana* is a perennial, in colder climates it must be treated as an annual and fresh seeds sown every spring. They are best sown indoors in boxes and only planted out (around 10–20cm (4–8in) apart) when the soil has warmed up. Keep them moist and free from weeds.

If you grow any of the other varieties, just cut them right back in autumn and they will reappear year after year and sometimes spread quite alarmingly. All origanums develop a better flavour if grown in soil rich in humus and nutrients.

Other varieties

Today there are a vast variety of origanums on the market, and if you wish to grow some of these hardy perennials (they make very pretty clumps) I suggest you get a root or cutting from a friend or even buy one or two small plants of each from your local garden centre. Even one plant will make a good showing after just one year. *O. vulgare* (wild marjoram) grows fairly tall (60cm/ 2ft) and has endless varieties: *O. v. variegata*, *O. v.* 'compact pink'

An old copper kettle makes an original container for this sweet marjoram. The herb is a little straggly through lack of light, but it does look very pretty.

Golden marjoram 'Crinkle leaf'.

Origanum vulgare laevigatum.

(short), *O. v. aureum* (golden), and
O. v. laevigatum. There is also a
bushy variety, *O. onites* (pot or
French marjoram), and *O. onites*
'crinkle leaf'.

History

Origanum is a native of Mediterranean countries and the name comes
from the Greek *oros* (mountain) and
ganos (joy). Traditionally, the herb
was a symbol of youth, beauty and
happiness. If grown on graves, it
ensured happiness for the departed;
bridal couples were crowned with
marjoram.

Our ancestors used it for polishing
furniture and it was one of the main
ingredients for washing-up water.
Birds are fond of origanum seeds, so
leave some for them in winter.

Preserving and main uses

Some of the origanums will give you
fresh leaves all winter, but you will
probably have to dry *O. majorana.* It
can also be deep-frozen.

It is one of the constituents of a
bouquet garni (parsley, thyme and
marjoram), which is used in endless
dishes. Use it also on its own with
fish, in salads, and in egg and cheese
dishes. Remember to add it at the
end of cooking so as to retain the
flavour better.

Wild marjoram.

Various marjoram leaves.

Golden marjoram.

Petroselinum crispum
Parsley, wild parsley, Italian, French or Hamburg parsley

Can be grown anywhere

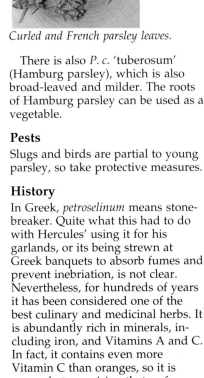

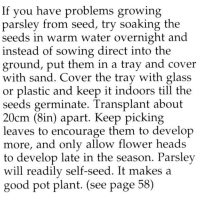

Petroselinum crispum.

Curled and French parsley leaves.

Family *Umbelliferae*

Biennial

Height: 35cm (14in)

Soil: Rich, deeply dug

Situation: sunny or partial shade

Propagation: seed

Main constituents: calcium, essential oil, flavonoids, iron, manganese, phosphorus, Vitamins A and C

Cultivation

Although parsley will grow for several years like a perennial, it will only yield its rich green leaves if treated as a biennial. Seeds are very slow to germinate and need warmth.

If you have problems growing parsley from seed, try soaking the seeds in warm water overnight and instead of sowing direct into the ground, put them in a tray and cover with sand. Cover the tray with glass or plastic and keep it indoors till the seeds germinate. Transplant about 20cm (8in) apart. Keep picking leaves to encourage them to develop more, and only allow flower heads to develop late in the season. Parsley will readily self-seed. It makes a good pot plant. (see page 58)

Other varieties

P. crispum 'Neapolitanum', known as wild, French or Italian parsley, is the broad-leaved variety, which, in *haute cuisine*, is considered to have a better flavour than the curly variety.

There is also *P. c.* 'tuberosum' (Hamburg parsley), which is also broad-leaved and milder. The roots of Hamburg parsley can be used as a vegetable.

Pests

Slugs and birds are partial to young parsley, so take protective measures.

History

In Greek, *petroselinum* means stone-breaker. Quite what this had to do with Hercules' using it for his garlands, or its being strewn at Greek banquets to absorb fumes and prevent inebriation, is not clear. Nevertheless, for hundreds of years it has been considered one of the best culinary and medicinal herbs. It is abundantly rich in minerals, including iron, and Vitamins A and C. In fact, it contains even more Vitamin C than oranges, so it is somewhat surprising that so far no food manufacturer has thought to make a drink from the herb, given our obsession, in the West, with buying endless cartons of orange drinks to keep away colds and flu.

Preserving and main uses

In mild winters, parsley can be picked fresh all the year, but it dries and freezes quite well. It is part of a bouquet garni and is used in countless dishes, both Western and Eastern.

Mixed herb bed showing French parsley, garlic chives, golden marjoram, curry plant (not in this book) and bergamot.

Pimenta dioica
Allspice, Jamaica pepper, pimento

Tropical climber: requires hot, humid greenhouse in colder climates

Family *Myrtaceae*

Tropical tree

Height: up to 12m (40ft)

Soil: rich, moist

Situation: hot and humid

Propagation: seed, cuttings, layering

Main constituents: volatile oil

Cultivation

Each berry on an allspice tree contains two seeds, which should be sown in warm, moist soil. Alternatively, take a cutting or layer an existing plant.

In temperate climates, allspice can be grown quite easily as an ornamental plant, but it will not flower unless a high humidity is maintained and the temperature never allowed to drop below about 18°C (65°F). Although it will grow up to 12m (40ft) in its native West Indies and South America, a tree of only 2–3m (7–10ft) will bear fruit in a greenhouse.

Although it is not difficult to grow as a plant, it is extremely difficult to get it to bear fruit, and it really flourishes best in its native Jamaica.

Other varieties

Another variety is *P. racemosa*, which is used to make rum.

History

Columbus discovered allspice in the West Indies, but because he was searching for the cloves, nutmegs and cinnamons already known to Europeans, he did not immediately recognise it as a valuable spice. It had been widely used by the Aztecs and Central Americans as a spice and to flavour chocolate.

The Spanish called it 'pimento' (pepper) because of its peppery flavour, and the French 'piment', a word which was also used for the fruits of the various capsicums. It is not, however, related to either of these, but to the East Indian clove.

The English naturalist John Ray eventually called it 'allspice' because of its resemblance to so many other flavours.

The early North American settlers used it in pumpkin pies, pickles and cakes. At one time, the United States and England almost destroyed the plantations because of a fashion for making walking sticks and umbrellas from allspice shoots!

Preserving and main uses

Pick fruit while still green and dry them in the sun or in a warm oven. Whole or in powdered form, due to its many-faceted flavours it can be used in a myriad of dishes both sweet and savoury: marinades, soups, stews, sausages, pâtés, curries, biscuits, and pies.

Allspice in flower growing in a hot, humid greenhouse. Note the palms.

Allspice.

Pimpinella anisum
Anise, aniseed

Half-hardy, requiring protection from frost

Family *Umbelliferae*

Half-hardy annual

Height: 30–40cm (12–18in)

Soil: alkaline and well–drained

Situation: sunny, protected from winds

Propagation: seeds

Main constituents: coumarins, glycosides, fixed and volatile oil

Cultivation

Anise is one of the few herbs that prefers an alkaline soil. It does not like being transplanted, so sow seeds in spring in position in the garden or in pots. Cover with 25–50mm (1–2in) of soil. Seeds can also be started under heat in pots. It is a graceful plant with fairly large first leaves and feather-like secondary ones. In a few months it develops a dainty head of white flowers. When these have set seed the whole plant should be cut and suspended for the seed to ripen. Bear this in mind when growing anise, for you can equally well use stem, leaves and flowers in cooking, as well as the seeds.

Other varieties

Illicium verum (star anise) is a tender tree originating in China, the star-like fruit of which has a flavour almost identical to anise. It is used similarly. It is not, however, related biologically in any way.

Star anise.

Pests and diseases

Slugs are rather fond of the delicate leaves, so take precautions. Mice are said to be irresistibly attracted to anise, although I have had not trouble from them. In fact, at one time anise was used as bait for mice!

History

Anise has been used medicinally and culinarily for many centuries by the Egyptians, Greeks and Romans. It probably originates from those countries. Pythagoras (in the sixth century BC) recommended it for warding off epileptic attacks. It was used, among other things, to cure coughs and indigestion, to keep features youthful, and also as a carminative, a diuretic, an aphrodisiac, and as a cure for halitosis!

The Romans, always pragmatic in what they did, used to make a special spiced cake, *mustaceus* (containing anise, cumin and other digestive spices), to add the finishing touch to their huge feasts.

Preserving and main uses

Dry the seeds and store them in airtight jars. Leaves and flowers are best used fresh.

Seeds can be used in a variety of breads and cakes, with fruit, and mixed into cream cheese, and are used in many savoury and curry dishes from the East.

Leaves and flowers can be added to salads. Anise is also used to flavour many liqueurs.

Large young anise leaves.

Anise seeds.

Anise in flower.

40

Piper nigrum
Black pepper, white pepper

Tropical climber, requiring hot and humid greenhouse in cold climates

Family *Piperaceae*

Tender perennial

Height: variable

Soil: rich in humus

Situation: hot, humid and shady

Propagation: Seed and cuttings

Main constituents: piperine, resins, starch, volatile oil

Cultivation

This is a climbing plant which originates from India, but is now grown extensively throughout Asia and Africa. You can grow it in a heated greenhouse where high humidity can be maintained. Grow either from seed or from a softwood cutting in rich soil full of humus. Provide a stake or another plant up which it can climb. In good conditions, it can reach 6m (20ft). If you are a keen spice-grower, why not grow it up a small nutmeg tree? This requires similar conditions and will provide the necessary shade. Keep moist at all times, but do not overwater.

Other varieties

P. longum and *P. officinarum* both come from India, too, and require similar cultivation. The latter ripens to a dark grey and is more pungent than *P. nigrum*.

History

In Indian literature, records of pepper go back at least 3,000 years. It was always a highly prized spice. As soon as it came to Europe, probably via Alexander the Great, it became the source of much fighting.

Branches of growing peppers.

The Visigoths, when besieging Rome in AD408, demanded 2.5 tonnes (2 tons) of gold and 2.5 tonnes (2 tons) of pepper as part of the price for sparing the city! Much later, European nations vied to find the source of pepper and establish plantations throughout the tropics.

Preserving and main uses

Both white and black peppercorns come from the same plant: indeed green and red ones, which are now also used, are just varying stages of ripeness on the same plant. Green

Pepper climbing up a tree.

peppercorns develop on grape-like bunches from insignificant white flowers and then turn red. Pick the berries when they are only faintly red to obtain black peppercorns. They should be dried as quickly as possible (preferably in full sun) to prevent mildew.

If you want white pepper, allow them to ripen completely, dry them, then soak them and remove the outer skin (pericarp). You are then left with 'white' peppercorns, which are milder than the black. You can grind fresh peppercorns in a mill at any stage of ripeness.

Keep the peppercorns in jars until required. Pepper is used in almost all savoury dishes according to taste.

Dried pepper-corns.

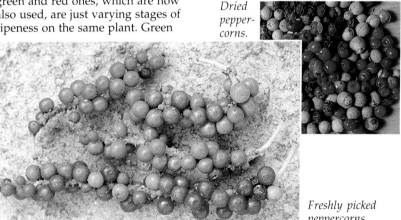

Freshly picked peppercorns.

Rosmarinus officinalis
Rosemary, compass-weed, polar plant

Can be grown anywhere

Rosmarinus officinalis.

Family *Labiatae*

Perennial

Height: 1m (3ft)

Soil: light, well-drained

Situation: sunny, sheltered from wind

Propagation: seed, cuttings, layering, division

Main constituents: acids, flavonoids, volatile oil

Cultivation

Rosemary seeds germinate very erratically, so if you are going to start off this way, I advise sowing seeds in boxes or a propagator where the temperature can be kept at 21°C (70°F) or above. Transplant into pots and then into final position.

Although hardy, rosemary will succumb to strong cold winds, so choose its position accordingly.

Cuttings of about 15cm (6in) in length can be taken in the latter part of the growing season from shoots that have not flowered. A mature bush will produce many layered plants.

The flavour of rosemary is stronger if it is grown on chalky soil.

Other varieties

These all need similar treatment to *Rosmarinus officinalis*:

R. o. prostratus, a low-growing variety with blue flowers that is much more susceptible to cold.

R. o. 'Miss Jessop's Upright' is hardy with white flowers.

R. o. 'Frimley blue' and 'Sudbury blue' are also quite hardy.

R. o. 'Albus' has white flowers.

History

Rosemary originates from Mediterranean countries. It was, and still is, widely used in medicines. It is also steeped in legend and symbolism. In Spain, it is revered because the bush sheltered the Virgin Mary on the flight to Egypt; in Italy it is said to ward off evil spirits. Brides wore it at weddings as it was the symbol of fidelity, but it was also used at funerals and other religious ceremonies.

It was said that 'where rosemary flourished, the woman ruled'.

Preserving and main uses

Use the leaves to flavour meat (especially lamb), poultry and fish, and also for sauces and potatoes. Use according to taste, but remember the flavour is quite pungent.

Leaves dry well, but fresh leaves can be gathered all year round.

Rosemary leaves.

Rosemary varieties growing in pots in a greenhouse.
Left to right: R. o. 'Miss Jessop's', R. o. prostratus, R. o. 'Albus',
R. officinalis, R. o. 'Frimley blue', R. o. 'Sudbury blue'.

Rumex acetosa
Sorrel, green sauce, sour sauce, Sally sour

Can be grown anywhere

Family *Polygonaceae*

Hardy perennial

Height: 60cm–1m (2–3ft)

Soil: rich and moist

Situation: any

Propagation: seed and division

Main constituents: oxalates, Vitamin C

Cultivation

Sorrel is easily grown from seed. Either sow in boxes and plant out or sow directly into the ground. It is an undemanding plant except for its requirement for water – it dislikes the soil drying out. Divide plants after a few years when clumps get too big.

Other varieties

R. scutatus, buckler-leaf sorrel or French sorrel, is a milder and shorter variety with rounder leaves. It is also less hardy than *R. acetosa*, and requires full sun and well-drained soil. *R. acetosella* (sheep's or field sorrel) grows wild in pastures all over the world and can be used like the other sorrels.

Pests and diseases

I have never known sorrel to suffer from any diseases, but slugs and snails can be a problem. They rarely ruin a whole plant, but watch out with seedlings.

History

No one quite knows the origins of sorrel; probably because it is so prolific and always grew everywhere, but it was used by the Romans.

It is a relative of docks, which become a nuisance, and which, unlike sorrel, are left untouched by domestic grazing animals. Finches are very fond of sorrel seeds.

People once believed an extract of sorrel would remove stains, and the ancient Chinese thought it could remove freckles.

Preserving and main uses

Use only fresh leaves. Sorrel neither dries nor freezes well. Do not use the very earliest leaves as they have much less flavour.

Use sorrel in salads, soups and sauces – pull out the centre stalks and discard them before chopping the leaves.

Sorrel leaves.

Common garden sorrel.

Salvia officinalis
Sage

Can be grown anywhere

Family *Labiatae*

Hardy perennial

Height: 30–60cm (1–2ft)

Soil: light, and slightly alkaline

Situation: full sun

Propagation: seed and cuttings

Main constituents: acids, flavonoids, tannin, volatile oil

Cultivation

Sow seeds direct in the ground or in boxes and plant out about 30cm (1ft) apart in a really sunny position and where the plants will get protection from winds. Cuttings strike easily and can be taken any time during summer. Renew plants after three or four years or when stems become very woody.

It is an extremely decorative plant, especially its numerous varieties.

Variegated sage.

Salvia officinalis 'tricolor'.

Other varieties

S. officinalis, which has grey-green leaves, has many colourful varieties, all of which will require similar cultivation:

S. o. 'purpurea', purple or red sage.

S. o. 'purpurea variegata', variegated purple sage.

S. o. 'Iterina', gold variegated sage (milder flavour).

S. o. 'tricolor'. Only half-hardy.

S. sclarea, clary sage, has pretty flowers, but grow it as a biennial.

S. elegans, pineapple sage, is half-hardy with pineapple-flavoured leaves.

History

A native of Mediterranean shores, sage has been a much-revered plant for centuries.

The Romans considered it a sacred herb, and an old Latin proverb said *'Cur moriatur homo cui salvia crescit in horto?'*, the meaning of which is 'Why should a man die when sage flourishes in his garden?' The word *salvia* comes from the Latin verb *salvere*, which means to cure, to save, or to be in good health.

In subsequent centuries, European sage became a prized export to the East.

Various types of clary sage (left and below). Clary sages make a very decorative addition to both herb gardens and mixed borders.

Salvia purpurea.

Mixed sage leaves.

Preserving and main uses

Pick leaves before flowers appear and dry in a cool place.

Use sage in stuffings and with rich meats. It can also be used to make sage vinegar and sage butter.

Satureia hortensis
Savory, summer savory

Can be grown anywhere

Family *Labiatae*

Annual

Height: 30cm (12in)

Soil: rich, slightly alkaline

Situation: full sun

Propagation: seeds

Main constituents: essential oil, resins, mucilage, tannins

Cultivation

Sow seed in spring and thin or transplant about 20cm (8in) apart. Keep cutting to encourage bushy growth, and, if drying leaves, harvest them just as the flowers begin to appear.

Summer savory.

Other varieties

The close relative of *S. hortensis* is *S. montana* (winter savory) and is well worth growing despite the fact that many consider its flavour inferior. It will grow in quite poor soil and requires less water than summer savory. Unlike summer savory, it is a perennial and if planted in a sheltered position, it will yield green leaves all the year.

Sow seed in spring or autumn or take stem cuttings in summer. Keep well trimmed to prevent growth becoming too woody.

History

Savories are natives of Southern Europe which soon spread to the North. They were one of the plants taken to North America in the seventeenth century by the early settlers. With its hot, peppery flavour, it was widely used until the advent of the more pungent spices from the East.

It was much used by the Romans, who believed it belonged to the satyrs (hence the name *Satureia*). Shakespeare in *The Winter's Tale* refers to '. . . mints, savory, marjoram . . . these are flowers of middle summer'.

Preserving and main uses

Leaves can be dried or frozen. Use (cautiously) in any dishes where you want a peppery flavour. Good in stuffings, sausages, and meat.

Savory is especially good with broad beans.

Winter savory (smaller) and summer savory leaves.

Sinapsis nigra
Black mustard
Sinapsis alba
White mustard

Can be grown anywhere

Family *Cruciferae*

Annual

Height: 1–3m (3–10ft)

Soil: any

Situation: sun or part shade

Propagation: seed

Main constituents: fixed oils, myrosin, mucilage, proteins, sinigrin

Cultivation

Mustards are one of the easiest plants to grow. A lot of people will remember growing white mustard together with cress in small boxes or trays on blotting paper. In fact, if you only want to use the leaves, this is probably the best way to grow them. They can be sown at short intervals so you always have a fresh supply. If, however, you want to harvest the seeds, sow liberally direct into the ground. They will germinate very quickly, but do not mix the seed of black and white varieties as their growth is uneven. Black mustard is stronger than white. Pick the seed pods before they open.

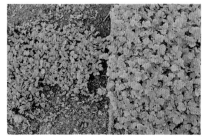

Mustard seedlings sown at the same time. Left: white. Right: black.

Black mustard pods.

White mustard pods.

Mustards also make a good green manure; that is, a plant that enriches the soil, so after harvesting the pods you can just fork in the remaining leaves.

Other varieties

S. juncea, brown mustard. Cultivation is similar to that of white and black, but the plant is smaller and the seeds do not preserve so well.

Pests and diseases

Like many *Cruciferae*, mustards seem to suffer badly from flea beetles (*Phyllotreta spp.*). Covering your sown patch with one of the very light transparent fleeces or nets now available on the market can help to keep them out, but some may have hibernated in the very patch in which you have sown the seed. If a covering fails and you are at your wits' end, use some derris powder, (an organic insecticide made from the roots of the Derris species). But like all insecticides, however organic, it can be harmful to beneficial creatures such as ladybirds and parasitic wasps. It will also kill fish, so keep it away from ponds.

White mustard.

History

For centuries, mustards have had all kinds of uses, both medicinal and culinary. Mustard seed is also the focus of one of the parables in the New Testament.

The Greeks and other Europeans had dozens of medicinal uses: for bruises, chilblains, rheumatism, epilepsy, snakebite and many more. The Romans mixed it with new wine. People were unknowingly correct in its widespread medicinal use, as the oil mustard contains is highly anti-fungal and anti-bacterial. Nowadays, mustard is mainly used as a condiment and in Asian dishes.

Preserving and main uses

Use fresh leaves and flowers in salads. Pick seed pods before they open and hang them up to collect the seeds. Use seeds in sauces and pickles and other dishes. Very sensitive skins can be irritated by mustard seeds.

Mustard seeds.

Thymus vulgaris
Thyme

Can be grown anywhere

Family *Labiatae*

Perennial

Height: 10–25cm (4–10in)

Soil: light, well-drained, neutral to alkaline

Situation: sunny

Propagation: seeds, cuttings

Main constituents: alcohols, flavonoids, saponins, tannin, volatile oil

Cultivation

Sow thinly directly into the ground or in boxes or pots and lightly cover with sand. When large enough to handle, plant out about 18–30cm

Thymus vulgaris.

(7–12in) apart. All the varieties of thyme love a sunny position and well-drained but not-too-rich soil, so choose your position carefully in relation to other plants. There are many varieties, all very decorative, so many people have a whole area devoted to thymes.

Keep the common thyme well trimmed so you get a nicely shaped bush. If you allow it to flower freely it will easily seed itself.

Thymes also make excellent pot plants.

Other varieties

There are dozens of varieties of thyme. Here are a few, all requiring similar cultivation:

T. album – a short variety with white flowers.

T. x citriodorus. Lemon-scented variety about 30cm (1ft) tall.

T. x citriodorus 'Archer's Gold'.

T. pulegioides. Bush variety with larger and stronger-flavoured leaves than *T. vulgaris*.

T. pulegioides 'Aureus'. A golden variety.

T. serpyllum. Creeping thyme.

T. serpyllum 'Coccineus'. Creeping variety with crimson flowers.

T. 'Fragrantissimus'. Orange-scented with blue-grey leaves; 38cm (15in) tall.

History

Thymes originate from the Mediterranean, where they used to grow wild everywhere, especially on the hillsides. I can remember literally wading through fields of wild herbs in Provence, but such delights are rapidly becoming rarer.

Thyme has inspired poets over the centuries, including Virgil and Shakespeare, while Kipling referred to 'thyme that smells of dawn in paradise'.

The Egyptians used it for embalming as it has strong antiseptic and preservative qualities. The Greeks (the name comes from the Greek *thymon*, courage) used it in baths

Mixed herbs make an attractive bed on their own. Paths are made of gravel with a stone edging. This bed consists solely of various varieties of thyme.

Thymus serpyllum coccineus.

Thymus x citriodorus 'Archer's Gold'.

Thymus serpyllum.

Thymus vulgaris variegata.

and anointed their bodies with it. Later, European ladies embroidered a sprig of thyme for their knights errant.

It was thought to enable one to see fairies, and Culpeper listed it as, among others, a cure for nightmares. The remedies, uses and stories are endless.

Preserving and main uses

Thyme can be collected fresh all the year round, except during really cold spells. Dry the leaves, or deep-freeze them in little bags.

Thyme is indispensable for all kinds of cooking, especially Mediterranean dishes, together with its bouquet-garni companions.

Thyme leaves.

Thymus album.

Trigonella foenum-graecum
Fenugreek, bird's foot, Greek hayseed

Requires protection from frost

Family *Leguminosae*

Tender annual

Height: 30–60cm (1–2ft)

Soil: any

Situation: sunny

Propagation: Seed

Main constituents: alkanoids, calcium, flavonoids, iron, oils, mucilage, saponin, Vitamins A, B and C

Cultivation

Although now mainly associated with curries and grown in Eastern countries, fenugreek can in fact be grown almost anywhere.

Sow seed directly into the ground (in northern climates as soon as the soil has warmed up). Seeds germinate readily and growth is quick. For leaves as well as seeds, sow at intervals throughout the summer.

Fenugreek can also be grown as a green manure and the leaves dug in to enrich the soil.

Other varieties

T. purpurascens, a British variety.
T. coerulea, a variety used in Switzerland to flavour cheese.

History

Trigonella comes from the Greek meaning 'three-angled', which describes the shape of its corolla, and *foenum-graecum* is the Latin for Greek hay. It has been used for centuries, not only in India, but also by the Egyptians, Greeks and Romans, as a spice, as a medicinal plant, and for cattle, who enjoy it mixed in their food.

Fenugreek is rich in all kinds of minerals and vitamins, which accounts for its many uses: the Chinese prescribe it for impotence and menopausal complaints; it was once thought to be an aphrodisiac;

Fenugreek pods ready for harvesting.

and it has been used to encourage lactation.

Preserving and main uses

Use fresh leaves in salads. Leaves can be dried. Pick pods before they open and store seeds for use whole in soups and chutneys, or, ground to powder, in curries. Before grinding seed, roast very slowly, either in a dry pan or in the oven.

Fenugreek seeds.

Fenugreek.

Zingiber officinale
Ginger

Requires hot, humid greenhouse in cold climates

Family *Zingiberaceae*

Tender perennial

Height: 1m (3ft)

Soil: rich in humus

Situation: hot, humid shade

Main constituents: amino acids, fats, minerals, oleoresin, proteins, starch, Vitamins A and B

Cultivation

In cold northern countries ginger was, until recently, considered an exotic Eastern spice, not easily obtainable fresh. Nowadays, it is widely sold and is relatively easy to grow.

It can be grown in pots or in the ground, providing the temperature never drops below 20°C (68°F) and the soil, which should be rich and well drained, is never allowed to dry out.

Plant a piece of fresh root about 25–50cm (1–2in) deep. It will soon produce tall pinnate shoots and the rhizomes will go on spreading indefinitely unless harvested.

Dig the roots up after twelve months or more and keep them in a cool dry place.

Ginger has attractive fragrant flowers, but these are very rarely seen. Fruits are seldom produced.

Other varieties

Alpinia officinarum (lesser galangal) and *A. galanga* grow in the same way as ginger. Their flavour is similar but milder.

Ginger growing outdoors in Asia.

History

Although ginger has been used for thousands of years, its origins are obscure. It was brought from China and Asia to Europe and America, where it has always been popular, being largely used in confectionery, gingerbread and ginger ale. The American revolutionaries of the eighteenth century were actually given ginger as part of their food ration!

Preserving and main uses

The roots can be kept fresh for quite a long time if left in a cool place (not the refrigerator, as this dries it out). They can also be dried and pounded into powder.

Ginger is widely used in Eastern dishes and curries and is delicious with fish.

Ginger growing in a pot.

Galangal roots.

Ginger roots in an Asian market.

Zyzygium aromaticum

syn. Eugenia caryophyllata

Clove

In cold climates requires a large heated and humid greenhouse

A sprig from a clove tree, showing the unopened buds ready for picking.

Family *Myrtaceae*

Tender tree

Height: 10–15m (30–50ft)

Soil: rich in humus, well-drained and slightly acidic

Propagation: seed or cutting

Main constituents: acid, caryophyllin, volatile oil

Cultivation

Clove trees come from the tropics of Asia and Africa, so in northern countries they must be grown in a greenhouse with plenty of humidity and some shade. Do not try it unless you really have plenty of room, because a clove tree will not bud until it is several years old and at least 2m tall (6ft or more).

Grow from seed (do not use the 'clove' sold for cooking), or, better still, from a cutting. As with all tropical plants, always keep it moist and never allow the temperature to drop below 21–25°C (70–77°F). A constant temperature of around 30–35°C (86–95°F) is best.

After a few years white flower buds will form and turn slightly yellow/pink. It is at this point, *i.e.* before they open, that they must be pinched out and dried. The flowers grow in clusters, but they do not all turn colour at the same time, so 'harvesting cloves' goes on most of the year.

Once the flower has opened do not harvest it but allow it to go on and produce its seed.

History

Clove trees originated in the Moluccas and were one of those prized spices that caused so much bloodshed: not only infighting among the Europeans, but often cruelty and massacre of local populations.

Cloves were chewed in China 2,000 or more years ago, primarily by courtiers or mandarins coming to consult the Emperor. A slave would offer a bowl of cloves at the entrance of the palace and by the time a visitor reached the Emperor his breath would be suitably sweet and pleasant!

In India and elsewhere, betel-nut chewers consumed (and some still do) vast quantities of cloves. Today, clove-flavoured cigarettes are still made in Indonesia and Malaysia.

Preserving and main uses

The dried bud will keep its flavour for many months if kept in an airtight jar.

You can use cloves in pomanders, pot-pourris and mulled drinks; while in cooking they are widely used in apple pies, curries, marinades, and teas, and also with ham, fruit, and to flavour many other dishes.

Leaves on a clove tree.

Dried clove buds ready for culinary use.

A variety of colourful herbs and spices.

Good organic gardening

Organic gardening is not a complicated science: it is merely imitating nature in a organised way. Herbs are undemanding and are probably the easiest plants to grow naturally. If you want to grow tropical spices in a temperate part of the world you will have to grow them in greenhouses or indoors; while anyone living in a hot, arid climate will have to provide water.

Herbs have been growing in the wild for thousands of years, and if you choose varieties that have not been genetically engineered you will have little or no trouble. In the wild, decaying plants and animal manures ensure that growing plants always have a good supply of nutrients, but in a cultivated garden you must provide these without using chemicals. The best way to do this is to make your own compost heap. This will provide a good source of food for your plants and enrich your soil, and also get rid of much of the 'rubbish' which would normally just fill up your dustbin.

Organic composts can be bought, but the cheapest and best way is to make your own. The following pages give some guidance on how to make a very simple compost heap. (If you want a more sophisticated compost heap using boxes, tumblers, etc., refer to the list of books inside the back cover.) If you have enough space, make two heaps – one for ready use, and one for new matter.

Hints on compost and weed control

1. You can put an activator in the centre of your heap, or mix it throughout. All organic matter will be broken down into compost whatever you do.

2. If using no-dig beds, spread compost on top of the soil every year. There is no need to dig it in, as worms will eventually take it down into the soil.

3. Fresh animal manure can also be put on top of beds, but do not put down too much or place it too close to plants, as it may burn them.

4. Fresh grass mowings (also hay and straw) can be put round plants to a depth of 5–8cm (2–3in) to keep out weeds. Even more effective is putting newspaper round plants and then covering it with hay, straw, or mowings. Water plants well first.

5. Remember that citrus peelings and trimmings from evergreens such as conifers and rhododendrons will make the soil acid.

6. Putting rotted leaves (leaf mould) on top of soil will help keep out weeds and will improve the structure of the soil, but does not add many nutrients.

7. Wood or bark chips, which can now be bought at good garden centres (unless you can make your own) are good weed controllers and look attractive.

8. If you own a shredding machine, any fresh leaves or hedge cuttings can be put on top of the soil once they have been shredded: they will also keep down weeds. (Any compost, even if it is not yet wholly rotted, can be dug into beds (see page 54)).

How to make a simple compost heap

Choose a corner of the garden for your heap or heaps. Compost is wonderful stuff, not smelly if managed properly but not exactly decorative. All you need is something to cover your heap (old carpet will do, or some black plastic, to keep in the heat and moisture), and plenty of organic matter.

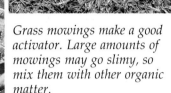

Grass mowings make a good activator. Large amounts of mowings may go slimy, so mix them with other organic matter.

ACTIVATORS

Any animal manures (horses, cows, chickens, pets, etc.) are wonderful for your heap. All activators, if put in the centre or mixed throughout the heap, will heat it up.

Nettles are a good source of nitrogen.

Cover heap with old carpet or black plastic.

Water before covering and keep moist.

DO NOT USE

Turn every few weeks. One small compost heap will contain billions of bacteria and soil creatures that will break down any organic matter.

Activators will heat your heap if put in the centre or mixed in, and will kill harmful pests and weeds.

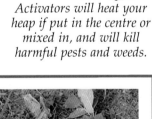

Plastic waste from any household is legion, but do not put any on your heap. Keep plastic trays for seed boxes, and small containers (cream, yoghurt, etc.) for potting on seedlings.

Do not use any kind of metal or glass.

Do not use any animal manures from intensive farms. They are likely to contain antibiotics, heavy metals and growth-promoters.

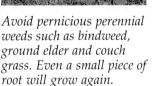

Avoid pernicious perennial weeds such as bindweed, ground elder and couch grass. Even a small piece of root will grow again.

GOOD INGREDIENTS

Weedings from your garden. Beware of seeds unless your heap heats up, because the seeds will germinate. Not a disaster, just more work!

Potato haulms or any vegetable debris from the garden are good.

Vegetable and fruit peelings are ideal. In fact, any organic kitchen waste can be put on your heap.

Sticks and stemmy materials will help circulate air.

USE IN MODERATION

Meat and fish scraps make good compost, but they may also attract mice, rats and flies.

Torn-up paper and cardboard can be used, but avoid printed coloured papers.

Brandling worms have marked rings, as shown here, and should not be confused with earthworms.

How to make 'worm compost'

If you have only a very small garden or are just growing herbs in boxes or pots, you can also make compost by using special brandling worms (not earthworms) in a bin. Brandling worms can be obtained from some organic garden centres, from heaps of stable manure or from angling shops. The latter usually have brandling worms in stock, as they are used for fish bait.

You can buy special containers for making worm compost, but an old plastic dustbin is perfectly adequate. If you want to keep the bin going, removing the compost can be a problem. I just dig out the ready compost and return as many worms as possible to the bin. Alternatively, you can spread out the contents on to newspaper and put a clump of wet paper in the middle. The worms will converge on the wet spot and the casts can easily be collected.

Water the surface if the mixture gets dry

Put a lid on the bin to keep flies out

Worms like to be warm, so keep the bin away from cold winds and frost

Cover the waste with newspaper to prevent any smell

Add a little chopped waste every day

Put the worms in some leaf mould or strawy manure

Place a board, with some small holes in it, on to the gravel

Drill holes near the bottom to let water escape

Put some gravel in the bottom

Pests and diseases

Herb and spice plants seem to suffer from relatively few pests and diseases, the common exception being their seedlings, which can be devoured by slugs, cutworms and other pests. The most important thing is that your plants have the right conditions. Light, plenty of food in the soil, water, drainage and temperature are all very important and if you observe these you should have little trouble.

At the time of going to press, a parasitic nematode had just come on to the market for controlling the organic gardeners' worst enemy, the slug. A godsend, but as yet expensive. I have tried it and it works brilliantly! Also, traps for slugs can be made by sinking small containers filled with beer or milk into the ground. Leatherjackets and other pests can be attracted to the surface by covering grass cuttings with wet cardboard or newspaper. Be careful that you only dispose of the pests! The best way, however, is to encourage pests' natural predators, such as birds, beetles, slow-worms, frogs and ladybirds.

Encourage as many natural predators of pests as possible, such as frogs, toads, beetles, slow-worms, hoverflies, ladybirds, and insectivorous birds.

The subject of diseases caused by viruses, fungi or bacteria is immense and difficult. Often the same outward symptom can have many different causes. For instance, leaves turning yellow and dropping off could be a sign of nutrient deficiency, lack of drainage, pests in the roots or a viral disease. Good management will keep most diseases and pests at bay. If you are sure your plants have a bad disease, the best course is to pull them up and burn them.

Greenhouse pests and diseases

When growing plants in a confined space and at a high temperature and/or humidity, it is even more important that you keep your plants strong and healthy by good management. In an enclosed environment pests and diseases can spread like wildfire and completely destroy crops.

It may sound 'quirky', but plants resemble humans in that if they are given the right environment and food, they will grow strong and healthy, well able to resist the onslaught of bacteria and viruses. Also, just as some humans have genetic deficiencies which make them prone to attacks of certain diseases, some plants that have been genetically engineered can be prone to attacks by all kinds of pests and diseases.

Experiment yourself. I had two turmeric plants in pots growing side by side. I did not keep one sufficiently watered. In no time it was covered with red spider mite and scale insects, whilst its neighbour remained strong and healthy.

If you spot a pest, take immediate action. You may be able to take advantage of modern biological control, which, in most cases, just means introducing the predator of a particular pest. These are available from specialist shops, although not yet, alas, from garden centres, which still seem to concentrate on pesticides.

Opposite you will find a list of the most common pests and their predators. When you 'buy' a predator, instructions are given on how to introduce it.

Hints on preventing pests and diseases

1. Pot on seedlings as soon as possible. Never allow them to get weak and straggly.

2. Do not allow temperatures to drop below those stipulated.

3. If plants are in pots, ensure good drainage.

4. Water correctly. Plants indoors must never be allowed to dry out. Spray leaves frequently.

5. Ensure good ventilation, but avoid cold draughts.

6. Constantly inspect plants for signs of trouble.

7. Any diseased plant should be quickly removed and burnt.

8. Pests, if spotted early, can be physically removed.

Biological control chart

PEST		BIOLOGICAL CONTROL	
	Aphididae Aphid		Introduce the midge *Aphidoletes aphidimyza*. Natural predators: ladybirds, lacewings, parasitic wasps, hoverflies
	Coccus hesperidum Scale insect	No biological control as yet. Can easily be wiped off with a soft wet cloth if spotted in time. Make sure plants do not dry out	
	Gastropoda Slugs		Introduce nematodes (*Phasmarhabditis* sp.) into the soil. The swollen slug on the left is infested with nematodes
	Lacanobia oleracea Tomato moth caterpillar	Spray with bacterium *Bacillus thuringiensis*. Also effective on other caterpillars in the garden	
	Lycoriella Sciarid fly		Introduce nematodes *Steinernema* sp. or *Heterorhabditis* sp.
	Otiorhynchus sulcatus Vine weevil		Introduce nematodes *Steinernema* sp. or *Heterorhabditis* sp.
	Phytomyza syngenesiae Leaf miner	Biological controls are now available: *Dacnusa sibirica* and *Diglyphus isaea*.	
	Pseudococcus obscurus Mealybug		Introduce *Crytolaemus montrouzieri,* a predatory ladybird
	Tetranychus urticae Red spider mite		Introduce predatory mite *Phytoseiulus persimilis*
	Trialeurodes vaporariorum Glasshouse whitefly		Introduce *Encarsia formosa,* a parasitic wasp

Propagation

There are three main ways of propagating herbs and spices: seeds, division, cuttings and/or layering. With the exception of some of the tropical tree spices, propagation by seed is the easiest.

Seeds

You can sow seeds straight into the ground, but I prefer to sow them in a box. Prick them out into pots and only plant them out when they are growing strongly. The main reason is that I find some herb seedlings seem to have a special attraction for slugs, snails, leatherjackets and the like. I have had whole sowings devoured by these pests!

You can make a good home-made seed compost: I use three parts loam, two parts well-rotted compost and two parts fine grit or sand.

As soon as you can handle the seedlings, either thin them out or pot on into small pots. There is no need to buy expensive plastic or clay pots – use some of the many plastic containers you would otherwise throw away every week: yoghurt pots, cream pots, cheese or pudding containers…Make some drainage holes in the bottom (a skewer is useful for this) and pop in your plants.

The compost used for potting-on can be stronger than that used for seeds, i.e. add more rotted manure or compost. If you plant out healthy, robust plants you will find they will survive even a slug onslaught. For some reason, self-sown plants seem to survive far better than those I sow straight into beds. Dill, parsley, coriander and caraway are just a few that I allow to seed themselves.

These are self-sown parsley seedlings that survived slugs, snow, and ice in their hundreds.

Potted-on seedlings in reused yoghurt pots.

Cuttings

You can take cuttings of the woodier herbs and spices such as rosemary, bay and some of the tropical tree and shrub spices. Cut sprigs when the plant's current year's growth has hardened and plant them in pots containing a compost similar to seed compost. Cuttings may take several months to root, but when they do, plant them out.

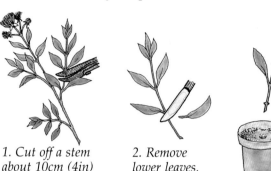

1. Cut off a stem about 10cm (4in) long.

2. Remove lower leaves.

3. Plant in compost.

4. A plastic bag helps keep in heat and moisture.

5. Once rooted, repot or plant out.

Division

This is probably the easiest method of propagation. Divide the bulbs or roots into two or more pieces and plant out.

Root crops such as ginger, turmeric and horseradish need to have a small piece broken off and planted about 25–50mm (1–2in) below soil level. Bulbs, such as those of chives, are better if divided every few years.

Herbs in pots, window-boxes and containers

Even if you have no garden at all, you can still enjoy the wonderful taste of fresh herbs in your cooking. They also make attractive pot plants in your home.

Almost all herbs can successfully be grown in containers, of which there is a vast variety on the market. Just make sure you give the plants sufficient light. Even if you live in a basement flat, fresh herbs need not be beyond your reach. There are now many electric bulbs and tubes on the market which will replace sunlight and give your plants all the light they require.

Drainage and correct watering is also important. Crocks or stones in the bottom of your container will help. If you do not have your own compost heap or worm bin, you will have to buy a good organic potting compost. You can now also buy a number of organic fertilisers and minerals which are good as top-dressings. Here are some of them:

Blood, fish and bone	Rock phosphate
Bone meal	Rock potash
Hoof and horn	Seaweed meal

If you have your own compost, here is a good mixture for pot plants: three parts loam; three parts compost; one part grit or sand; some leaf mould if available.

Most plants will last two or three years in the same pot if given a good annual top-dressing of compost or organic fertiliser.

Bronze fennel makes an attractive pot plant but can grow very tall.

The fresh green leaves of lemon balm look attractive in a terracotta bowl.

More pictures of herbs in pots and containers can be found on pages 12, 19, 20, 34, 35, 36 and 42.

Thyme in a strawberry pot.

Designing a herb bed

Layout

Herbs can be planted in clumps anywhere in your garden or in conventional rows. Personally, I prefer to put as many as possible in one bed near the kitchen (handy for picking), and preferably without too much hard work digging or weeding. To achieve this, deeply dig a bed, preferably to two-spade depth, and leave the soil to one side. (Make sure you can comfortably reach to the middle of the bed, or the back of it if it is against a wall or fence.) Refill bed with soil and compost, making a kind of sandwich, *i.e.* compost – soil – compost – soil. Providing you do not walk on it, a bed like this need not be dug again for many, many years. I have had herbs growing in the same bed for nearly ten years and have never dug it during that time – just weeded it occasionally, and added more compost from time to time.

If you intend having only one herb bed, first decide which herbs you wish to grow and plan the layout carefully, taking into account the eventual height of the plants, whether they like full sun or not and whether they will have to be replaced every year. Here are some suggested layouts:

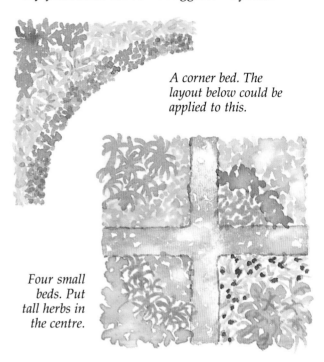

A corner bed. The layout below could be applied to this.

Four small beds. Put tall herbs in the centre.

Fennel · Bay tree · Borage · Lovage · Sweet cicely · Angelica · Lemon balm · Dill · Rosemary · Mints · Sage · Caraway · Garlic · Savory (winter & summer) · Chervil · Chives · Basil · Tarragon · Mustard · Origanums · Parsley · Thyme

A simple single bed. Make sure you can reach the back if it is against a wall.

Designs for herb gardens.

Formal designs for herb gardens

If space is no problem, you may want a whole area devoted to herbs, incorporating several beds. Here are some medieval designs for herb gardens. Remember, this book deals only with culinary herbs: medieval gardens would certainly have had aromatic and medicinal herbs as well. You may wish to grow these too, but they are not included in this book.

Also, there is really nothing to stop you inter-cropping culinary herbs with some of your favour-ite flowers or vegetables, as long as you bear in mind the plants' individual requirements for sun and shade. If you have only a small 'patch' in a town garden, just think how attractive one of these designs would look! Paths round these formal designs are best bricked or made of stone or gravel, but these may be expensive. Wood-chip or bark paths are a cheaper alternative. Line paths with old newspaper or carpet first to help keep out weeds.

Edgings round beds can be made of wood, brick, or other materials which are available from garden centres.

61

Preserving herbs and spices

Nothing can really replace a fresh herb or spice in cooking, although many of the seeds and roots retain their flavour very well. However, not all herbs grow all the year round and often it is just not practical to use everything fresh. There are several ways of preserving them.

Drying

The commonest way of preserving any herb or spice is by drying. Leafy varieties are the most difficult. Warmth and air are essential, so a dry shed, airing cupboard or somewhere in the kitchen would be ideal. I use my range stove, which dries them very quickly. Sun is not always good as it can bleach out colour and flavour. Either tie the herbs in bundles and hang them up, or spread them on a tray in a warm place. As soon as they are completely dry, put them in airtight jars. Do the same

with the seed varieties such as mustard, caraway and fennels (but do not use artificial heat). Those in pods have to be dried in their pod, then threshed with a tray underneath or shelled and stored, *e.g.* fenugreek and mustards. It is a good idea to put a tray underneath any herbs with seeds so that none go to waste on the floor. Many roots or corms such as ginger, turmeric and garlic will keep a long time in a dry cool place anyway.

Freezing

Leafy herbs are suitable for freezing. Put them in small freezer bags, but put only as much as you would use in one go in each bag and freeze that.

Although I have not covered herbs for drinks, teas and infusions in this book, a nice 'trick' is to serve up drinks, alcoholic or non-alcoholic, on cold snowy winter days with apparently completely fresh herbs. Just put a sprig of one or two leaves into your ice-cube tray and pop the cube in your drink. Mint, lemon verbena and lemon balm are particularly suitable. Anyone who lives in the tropics does not have to resort to such subterfuge!

Herbs can be dried in a shed or garage.

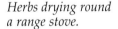

Herbs drying round a range stove.

Glossary of constituents by Gwilym Swift MRCVS

Acids	Substance combines with alkali to form salt/sour taste. Blue litmus turns red. Organic acid such as vinegar and lemon juice. Inorganic acid poisonous in excess.
Albumen	Proteins resembling egg white. All easily precipitated in digestive processes.
Alcohol	Product of fermentation of sugars. Can dissolve many substances, including alkaloids.
Alkaloids	Active principle of plants which can form salts with acids.
Amino acids	Protein molecule derived from ammonia.
Asparagain	A white crystalline amino acid found in many seeds.
Basil camphor	Aromatic camphoraceous oil.
Calcium	Metallic element which will combine with acids such as chalk and plaster of Paris.
Capsaicin	Red colour from cayenne pepper (capsicum).
Carotenoids	Pigments of a class including carotene (orange or red).
Caryophyllin	Monoterpinoid found in buckwheat and sorrel.
Cineol	Diterpenoid found in eucalyptus species (globulus labill).
Coumarins	Aromatic substance found in seeds of tonka bean, etc.
Crocin	Carotenoid found in such species as *Saffron naturilis*.
Circumin-curcumene	Sesquiterpeniod found in turmeric colouring.
Essential oil	Volatile oil, aromatic, evaporates quickly.
Fixed oil	Non-volatile oil.
Fats	Natural ester of glycerol and acid.
Flavonoid	Flavine derivative. Yellow dye of alkaloid.
Gallotannin	Derivative of tannic acid. Astringent, bitter substance.
Gum	Soluble viscous exudate. Complex molecule from stems or branches of trees.
Hyssopin	Aromatic oil with healing properties.
Iron	Metallic element combines with acid to form ferric/ferrous salts.
Magnesium	Metallic element of the alkaline earths. Essential salts in organic growth in plants (chlorophyll).
Manganese	Metallic trace element.
Marrubiin	Bitter aromatic oil used in cough remedy.
Minerals	Inorganic substances – salts of elements.
Mucilage	Viscous substance from plant seeds. Solution of gum acacia/tragacanth. Helps to keep particles in suspension.
Myrosin-myrsine-myrsellin	Coumarin substance from myrtopsis species.
Oleoresin	Essential oil/resin mixture, *e.g.* balsam.
Oxalate	A salt of oxalic acid (wood sorrel and other plants, *e.g.* rhubarb leaves).
Phosphorous	Non-metallic element in allotrophic form – basis of phosphates.
Piperine	Volatile oil similar to morphia found in *Piper nigrum*. Aromatic stimulant and carminative.
Potassium	White soft alkaline metallic element. Combines readily with oxygen. Essential in fruit and flower development.
Proteins	Organic, nitrogenous compounds constituent of plant foods.
Saponins	Glycoside (sugar derivative) causing foaming.
Sinigrin	Crystalline glycoside of black mustard seeds. Precursor of oil of mustard after action by enzymes.
Sodium	Similar to potassium. Alkaline metallic element. Essential salts.
Sugar	Carbohydrate group or organic molecules with CHP constituents.
Starch	Amylose group of carbohydrates converted to sugar in presence of dilute acid.
Sulphur	Non-metallic element. Crystalline or amorphous with medicinal properties.
Tannin	Non-crystalline pale-yellow powder soluble in water and glycerine.
Thymol	White crystalline aromatic hydrocarbon derivative from oil of thyme.
Vitamin A	Carotene found in plants, fish oils. Oil-soluble.
Vitamin B	Water-soluble vitamin group found in plants, seeds, egg yolk, vegetables and fruit.
Vitamin C	Water-soluble ascorbic acid found in fruit juices; similar to citric acid.
Volatile oil	See essential oil.

Bibliography

Bremnes, Lesley, *The Complete Book of Herbs*, Dorling Kindersley, London, 1988

Culpeper's Complete Herbal and English Physician, J. Gleave & Son, Manchester, 1826

Garland, Sarah, *The Herb & Spice Book*, Weidenfeld & Nicholson, London,1979

Grieve, M., *A Modern Herbal*, Jonathan Cape, London, 1931

Holton, J.A., and Hylton, H. (eds), *The Complete Guide to Herbs*, Rodale Press, Aylesbury, 1979

Mabey, Richard (ed.), *The Complete New Herbal*, Penguin, London, 1988

Roberts, Margaret, *Growing Herbs with Margaret Roberts*, Southern Book Publishers (Pty) Ltd, S. Africa, 1985

Swahn, J.O., *The Lore of Spices*, Crescent Books, New York, 1991

For a list of books on organic gardening, see the inside back cover.

Index